Bloom Where You Are Planted

by Stevie Wilberding
& Beau Wilberding
as told to Meg Bertini

DreamTime Publishing, Inc.

DreamTime Publishing, Inc., books are available at special quantity discounts for bulk purchases for sales promotions, premiums, fund-raising, and educational needs. Please contact us at **www.DreamTimePublishing.com** for additional information.

Library of Congress Cataloging-in-Publication Data

Wilberding, Stevie.
Bloom where you are planted / Stevie and Beau Wilberding.
 p. cm.
ISBN 978-1-60166-017-6 (trade pbk.)
 1. Wilberding, Stevie—Travel. 2. Voyages and travels. I. Wilberding, Beau.
II. Title.
 G465.W535   2009
 910.4—dc22

                                    2009010102

Branding, website, and cover design for DreamTime Publishing by
 Rearden Killion • www.reardenkillion.com
Text layout and design by Gary A. Rosenberg • www.garyarosenberg.com

This publication is designed to provide accurate and authoritative information in regard to the subject matter covered. It is sold with the understanding that the publisher is not engaged in rendering legal, accounting, or other professional service. If legal advice or other expert assistance is required, the services of a competent professional person should be sought.

*—From a declaration of principles jointly adopted by a committee of the
American Bar Association and a committee of publishers.*

*This book is printed on recycled, acid-free paper containing
a minimum of 50% recycled, de-inked fiber.*

Contents

To Stephen Van C. Wilberding

*Sometimes a man walks into your life with dreams
so creative they take your breath away.
I am still gasping.*

With love and abundant thanks for the good ride.

Acknowledgments

There are too many people to thank.

Thank you Steve Wilberding, Dad, for your patronage, understanding and sense of adventure.

Thank you Ashley for the music in your soul.

Thank you Van for not only listening, but for *really hearing* what was being said.

Oh, and thanks also for suggesting that Mom write this book.

Thank you Onnie. If God made a nicer person, I don't know who it would be.

Thank you, Meg Bertini, for sharing our burden and bringing Mom's vision to fruition. You are good.

Thanks to Dr. Gordon and the incredible team of medical professionals who were able to help Mom to live those extra months. Not just survive them, but *live* them. Each moment was a gift.

To the hundreds of people who were there in person,
or there on the phone,
or there with an e-mail or card,
or there to hold Mom's hand,
or there to hold one of our hands,

or there with baked goods,
or there with a prayer,
or there because you'd planned on it a year ago,
or there just because you felt like being there. . . .
You know who you are.

Thank you.

Preface

elcome to my world of living abroad with all the hidden booby traps of an al-Qaida patrol. One learns to smell an inconvenience about to turn into catastrophe and sweet talk your innocent way out of it, resort to tears, or pull rank. The rule is, if you think there is a problem then there is one. And when the native answers your request with "No problem" that is the signal for the test-drive dummy in your head to put on the brakes.

I have planned to write this book for almost five years. It took about three years to get a true timeline on paper from which to work. There is some procrastination time-padding the project, as well as false starts, tentative material passed around the family, and then we found my aggressive terminal illness. No one in the family suggested I give up this book; after all I was already steeped in a family research project and was bringing an earlier book into the public domain. In fact, our family council of war determined that I invite Beau, my youngest son, to be a co-author as he was there for most of the events and he seems to bring forth the immediacy of life in his writing. Welcome aboard, Beauberding.

I decided I needed another writer to bring this travel project to life. Meg Bertini arrived the next week armed with the doggedness of a lawyer, the secrecy of a ghostwriter, the particularity of a publisher, and the drama of a Vegas headliner. I had my soul mate. Meg was amazed at the list of American staples just not available in foreign countries. But Beau was quick to point out that even if you had a year's supply to bring with you to Saudi Arabia from home, leave it at home because it might be confiscated. A classmate of his had shopped only at Sears for her clothes for the year. When they got to immigration and customs, the officer dumped it all in the bin as Sears was a blacklisted "Zionist" company. Cranberry juice cocktail was confiscated not because of the word cocktail . . . but juice (say it fast).

Today the list has been abandoned, but the message is still valid. Ashley and Van have been excellent contributors, as has Steve. It is difficult to imagine doing all this without them.

This isn't a chronology, but a knitting basket full of memories. We hope that our knitted experiences of letting go, digging in, and ferreting out will help you find many memories in your life.

Stevie Wilberding
Casey Key, Florida
September 2008

Introduction

From a traveler and art historian who's been to more than two hundred countries, who's lived abroad more than half of her life, and who's raised three children while doing so, comes a book that helps us understand how to excel no matter where you are. Stevie Wilberding, explorer extraordinaire, shares her experiences about what home is and how you can find it—and success—no matter where you are.

"Home" can mean an African roundel or a French château, but ultimately we all want to find success and happiness no matter where we are. What are the qualities that make up that solid feeling that all is well, even when you've known more than twenty structures as home, and have spent countless nights in hotel beds, not to mention on planes, trains, and automobiles? How do you bloom regardless of where your home du jour is?

We can learn much about this sense of "home" that we can use in our lives, even if we've never ventured more than fifty miles past the structure we ourselves grew up in.

There is a huge difference in living in a country and merely visiting. Many a traveler, for example, journeys through Japan without ever needing to realize that rice and salt generally cannot be purchased at a grocery store. When you pack a picnic as you travel that will be one lesson you will learn—probably the hard way.

Once you are an experienced traveler, though, your sense of perspective—as well as adventure—broadens, and you will experience things even on a shorter trip that many others would not, so anecdotes from her shorter trips are included here, too. Important to note is that the experiences related here are from a family who agrees that grabbing life with gusto is critical to blooming. Thanks to packaged tours and the American franchises that penetrate practically every crevice of the world, it is possible to leave home and experience nothing. That is certainly not what this book is about.

To some, the notion of following your spouse overseas for work, let alone raising a family that way, seems quaint. With today's technology and more modestly priced flights, one spouse can work overseas and still presumably maintain a good family relationship while the family never leaves the United States. Stevie, though, did travel with her husband, and if her family could bloom in Tokyo and Saudi Arabia before the days of the Internet, then certainly the rest of us can do so. At least once she points us in the right direction.

Meg Bertini

ONE

We're All Terminal

In the long run we are all dead.

—John Maynard Keynes

The New York Times crossword puzzles had certain rules in the '70s: you didn't use the word "cancer," for example. The puzzles were a diversion from reality, and the editors didn't want to worry their patrons. Today, on the other hand, "cancer" and worse appear regularly. That is very New York: direct, no frills, get the job done—with an attitude of mild scorn and a hint of abuse.

So now I'm on Casey Key, outside Sarasota, Florida, a newly minted cancer patient, wishing for the old rules. Today I canceled our Peru trip. In June we will not fly over the Nazca Lines, sail on Lake Titicaca, bird on the Amazon, nor walk Machu Picchu. Damn. I hate missing that. In October we will miss the great carpet cities of Isfahan and Qum and ruins of Persepolis.

"It seems like such a natural progression," I told Ashley, as we had our daily conversation about my impending departure. "Death seems so close to life, not a mysterious distant fog. Many old friends and family will be there, and if you are a busybody like me on earth you are bound to be that way as a spirit—finding my way back to the side of the living to see what's happening and how I can affect events. You will be visiting a TV program of a seer and he will say to you: 'There is a woman in a green hat standing next to you.' 'Oh, that's Mom,' you'll say. 'Well, she thinks you should put the couch back where it was and repaint the front hall lemon yellow.'" So it is each time laughing through tears that we get further into the understanding of how Ashley will get by with my being on the other side.

Today I said to Ashley, "You have become me."

She said, "I know. Are you mad?"
"No, I am always very proud of you."
In the weeks that come she will be prepared for my death.

Van just sits and looks miserable and says, "Don't die, Mom." I will need more time with Van cracking the outer shell of my former army tough guy. This is not a job which can be done with cool impassion.

Beau enters any room I am in, talking a mile a minute, cookie in hand looking for pillows and a rug to pull over me. He now does this without thinking about it. He holds me close ten times a day, blows kisses, rubs my back, and reminds me of yet another favorite moment we shared. When he isn't here he wallpapers my cell phone with messages of "I love you." He studied sociology in college and had an excellent if abrupt encounter with every aspect of dying. Yet, he too feels he has to apologize for past poor behavior. "Mom, I want to apologize for being such an a**hole from eighteen to twenty-two." To which I respond, "But darling, that was your job. To be an a**hole." He laughs and feels vindicated. I gotta say eighteen was a lot of years ago . . . He was no worse than his brother and sister.

The other day in the doctor's office I said to Steve, "This could be my last day."

"I know and I am so glad you are taking this in a cool and calm way," he replied.

I think he wouldn't be able to handle tears and fear from me. He only wants to talk about the practical details. We had the cremation people in and signed up. As I collect blue-and-white Ming porcelain, I particularly liked the idea of being put in the sea in a blue-and-white low-fired ceramic pot that floats for a minute and then melts.

It reminds me of the Ganesh festival in Bombay where little low-fired ceramic statues of Ganesh were placed in the bay after the celebration. But I said I can't go to church in such a poor pot; I must be at the memorial service best dressed in a Ming vase. So the contract was written that my ashes would be transferred to a Ming pot for the service and back into the blue-and-white ecologically sound one for burial at sea. We both felt accomplished and elated after that decision.

Then we discussed everyone wearing hats to the service. And again a radiant smile came to Steve's face. He gains in comfort as more decisions are taken. I tell him I am giving my jewelry to Ashley and our sons' wives now so I can see their beauty more radiant before I leave, and anyway, it's not for the second wife. I repeat that he shouldn't be stupid about choosing a second wife.

There is no practice for death. Each one is different. It is hardest for those who are left behind. These are the trite phrases I know are true. There is only the knowledge that we shall all be in heaven together one day. My prayer is, "Please, God, give me the wisdom to say the right comfortable words to my friends and family." Perhaps it too is selfish: I want them to release me with joy.

Clockwise from left: Ashley, Beau, Van, Stevie, Onnie,
in Madrid, Spain, Christmas 1988.

Impending death is a great conversation stopper. Very few people know what to say to someone who is dying. I also dare say that those of us who are dying don't really know what to say either. Throughout the world of all the awkward conversations I've had about politics, religion, and money, I'd vote for "death" the most awkward of all.

From my perspective, the awkwardness comes from not wanting to make others uncomfortable, yet not wanting to make myself uncomfortable by ignoring the pachyderm sitting on the couch. Added to that is my desire to make sure close friends, and even more so my family, are comfortable and at peace with my dying. This is no easy task when people don't even want to discuss it.

From being on the other side of the conversation, I know I've always had concerns about saying the right thing. Now, of course, I know that sometimes saying the right thing means saying nothing at all, but in a comfortable way, not in a way that you squirm in your chair.

I know it's also uncomfortable to talk about, because the death of others reminds us in an uncomfortable way that we, too, shall die. At twenty years old, this isn't as much of a problem. When we start hitting sixty or seventy years old, people start fleeing the room. "Oh, I think I left the coffee pot/iron/stove on. I must be going now."

I had the interesting luck as a child to be exposed to death quite frequently, so I think I've always been more comfortable around it than others have. As Onnie, my mother says, "Death is an old friend." When I was a wee girl, mother was pregnant with a little baby I named Nancy Susie Rosie. I truly felt she was my baby, but she never came home. I was very sad about that, but my family did not feel children had legitimate grief, so for years I mourned "my" baby alone.

Years later, when we brought Beau home from the hospital, Ashley said with great seriousness, "This is my baby." I understood she had formed a great attachment through the expectation of his arrival, and I respected it. She was a good mommy coming to me in the night saying, "Baby need didey." We weren't so keen, however, that she taught Beau to climb the stairs alone at six months!

My mother only had two children who lived—my elder sister Joan and I. Joan was killed in the famous Lake Pontchartrain plane crash in 1964 at the age of twenty-three. She was returning to her job at Chase Manhattan Trust Department, newly engaged to be married, and with an offer of a place at Tulane Law School.

Joanie had always been the star of the family. Who said so? Everyone. With Joan's death, I felt I was the poor specimen left behind and had to do something to make my family proud. My sister's success before her death spurred me on to my future accomplishments. One of her last lessons was **"The harder you hit me, the higher I bounce."** It served me well for many years.

As the years passed I have read much about near-death experiences and how those on the other side are part of our lives here. This has all blended in with my Episcopalian faith, rightly or wrongly. The outcome is a pleasant expectation of returning to the presence of my beloved grandparents and my sister, all of whom will have lessons for the new girl, no doubt.

Beau's Perspective

Mom was convinced she would lose at least one of us, and I think that greatly affected her outlook and philosophy in how she brought us up. She lived in fear of one of us getting run over or killed in some way because that was the reality of Mom's young life: she had four siblings, none of whom made it past her twentieth birthday.

She balanced knowing that we needed our space against fearing for our safety. This is true for all parents, but seems exacerbated in the case of Mom: international, high-risk living, with death a recurring theme when she was young.

Onnie mourned the losses of Mom's siblings, and onlookers saw Onnie as the primary sufferer. Mom was seen, perhaps, as a bystander to the grief, and not an active participant. This was not the case, though. Mom grieved for each of them, and missed her equal share of the consolation.

Death happens everywhere

Naturally from our time living overseas, I had abundant opportunity to see and share in the customs and rituals of other cultures. As it turns out, death is as difficult, if not more difficult, a topic in other places as it is here in the United States. Navigating the cultural differences that arise in death creates copious paperwork, real logistical headaches and some darkly humorous situations.

One of the major oil companies regularly brought their executives to Saudi Arabia in their corporate 747 jet, which requires two pilots. Passengers and pilots all had visas from the Saudi government as required. On departure, the Saudis cancel the visas in their passports. Unfortunately, one of the two pilots had a major heart attack on take-off, and the plane requested to return to the airport. The crew and passengers had to wait for a second pilot and were given rooms in a hotel. The problem was the dead body. The company didn't have permission to bring in a corpse, and he was illegal as baggage, and he was not alive to get a visa. The negotiations lasted all day, and finally accommodations were made at the morgue until the plane left a few days later.

Without a major oil company involved, we learned these things can take even longer when death causes a chaotic situation. Our old Ethiopian cook, Milky, moved with us into town when we relocated from the mud palace in Dir'aiyah. He had asked to buy the refrigerator and the locker freezer, which he was planning to take home with him to Ethiopia to start a restaurant. Unfortunately we caught him drunk—having finished up everyone's glass of wine at a dinner party—and we fired him and his illegal nephew, the grandson of Haile Selassie.

Milky died a few weeks after leaving us, but his employment papers still read that he worked for us. Steve and a fixer (a helpful chap who figures out drivers' licenses, passports, and random issues such as this) spent days negotiating the return of Milky and his possessions back to Ethiopia while he was kept in the comfort of the cooler. Several thousand dollars later, Milky, his side-by-side refrigerator, and locker freezer left on a plane for home.

Death of the Saudi king

When the king of Saudi Arabia died, he received the same burial as his servants received. He was wrapped in white sheets, put in the back of a pickup truck with his male relatives seated around him, and before the first nightfall was driven into the desert for burial in an unmarked grave, placed on his side facing in the direction of Mecca. Other Muslims in other countries, though, have the tradition of building very opulent tombs, which illustrates the wide range of beliefs and practices that exist within the Muslim faith.

For days after the king's death, friends visit the widow and daughters, bringing food and good company. The widow then waits to see how successful she can be in getting permissions from the new head of household—her eldest son—whom she spoiled while raising him, so that he will hopefully always treat her affectionately in return.

Princess Diana

When Princess Diana died in the car crash in Paris, we were living in Mumbai. Like the rest of the world, we tuned to the TV commentary, which produced every detail day and night. The Prince of Wales, and the princess' two sisters, arrived in France to take the princess back in his plane. With much ceremony she was given honors at the French airport. Not so when she arrived on English soil. My Parsi friend Piloo, who grew up in London, called me in shock. "What are they thinking? They have just put her in a hearse, and she is going *alone* to wherever?"

I must say it was awkward trying to explain the abandonment. When Parsis die, they are never alone from the moment of death until they are put in the Towers of Silence where the bodies are exposed to the sun and birds of prey. The Parsis see this as a final act of charity, giving nourishment to birds. The family members take turns sitting with the corpse, whispering in its ear and reliving precious memories with the departed. On the other hand, explaining the Towers of Silence was also difficult. We had friends whose apartment was close to the towers and not infrequently they found human toe and finger bones that the vultures dropped onto their terraces.

The cremation ceremonies, though, of the British also seem surprisingly harsh to the uninitiated. The coffin rests on a sort of railroad track in front of the altar. At the end of the service, the curtains part on one side and the coffin rolls into what one believes are the jaws of an actual furnace. Floral arrangements with personal sentiments from well-wishers accompany the coffin, implying the dearly departed sits up to read the notes after everyone has left.

Death rituals, though, give us, in subsequent generations, clues as to our roots. Steve and I visited Melrose Abbey in the Scottish Borders not long ago to see the ancient walls and filigree built by my ancestors, the Meins, a long line of stonemasons. The graveyard beside the abbey contains the remains and stone markers of many Meins: *Here lyis Androv Mein, meason port. In Newstead sum tyme callit vas. died 1624 at age 63* is the earliest we found.

Several generations of maps show locations of the stones moved many times over. My Australian cousin and close friend (though we have never met in person), Glenice Mein, explains with disgust that the headstones were moved to accommodate lawn-mower widths and other practicalities of upkeep!

Foreign can be in your own backyard

Being from the Northeast, and emotionally reserved Episcopalians, we were taken by surprise by the Baptist funeral of our dry cleaner, Luther, of Dahlonega, Georgia. The loud widow's wails "Oh, Luther, don't leave me. Come back," were incredibly uncomfortable for us. Other female relatives shouted out as well in an unashamed, emotional tirade. Just two days after delivering my first child, and going through my own emotional changes very quietly and privately, it was a real shock for me. In fact I was numb from the emotion. We later learned that the numbers and decibels of the shouting-out were compared with other funerals and one had to perform to measure up.

Final Thoughts from Stevie

Even though I am dying, I don't know any more about death than anyone else. I can say, though, that honest conversation is a great comfort to my children and friends. Talking about the weather passes the time, but it won't take the lump from your throat. If you find yourself or a loved one in my position, try to find out what is bothering those closest to you. Try to say those things that you would regret not saying. Don't force anything, but use your intuition. You know your loved ones better than anyone: use what you know to create a sense of personal peace for yourself and for others.

Stevie in her wedding hat at the wedding of great friends
Lucy and William Cromwell, Summer 1997.

Stevie and Steve on their way to a New York City wedding, Christmas 2007.

TWO

Toilet Paper

*"When one's expectations are reduced to zero,
one really appreciates everything one does have."*

–Stephen Hawking

Anyone who has traveled out of the country, even to Western Europe just a few years ago, knows exactly what I mean by this. Toilet paper. A simple resource in the United States, where the biggest dilemma you face is figuring out just how soft you want it. Overseas, in some countries, you are lucky even to find it, especially in public restrooms.

Many things we take for granted in the United States are like that, giving you fresh perspective and appreciation for all we have in the States when you return home. In Britain, an egg salad sandwich is a slice of egg with lettuce, not the concoction with mayonnaise we are used to here (ditto with chicken, by the way). What we call Jello they call jelly. What we call jelly is called jam. Mufflers there are bosoms here. So beware the consequences of asking for a new muffler in Oxford. Most of us have heard of the English knocking on your door as "being knocked up."

Privacy on the phone is something we Americans take for granted, but elsewhere, it is not the case. Fortunately, technology has improved so it's unlikely you'll have a voice break quietly into your conversation and ask "Please don't say anything while I change the tape" as my friend Sandra once did in Saudi Arabia.

Beyond the silly and relatively inconsequential (although anyone who's had a bout of traveler's stomach would dispute putting toilet paper into that category), more significant issues surface, especially once you reside abroad, rather than just visit. Speaking of which, our family is of the opinion that there are three *worst* places on earth to eat poisonous food. These places warn against: Delhi Belly, Mummy Tummy, and Montezuma's Revenge. Defensive eating is cooked chicken—that's one thing every non-vegetarian society can cook well.

Politics

Voting while living overseas used to be a true challenge, although recently they've been improving the process. In the 1970s and 1980s, though, the U.S. House and Senate presumed that anyone living overseas was a wandering backpacking hippy probably on drugs, and they did nothing to support those of us Americans living abroad. They were immune to the fact that we were bringing in foreign money, repatriating the U.S. dollar, disbursing American goodwill, and paying a lot of extra school fees, taxes, and flights home in order to be doing our country's work abroad.

The board for the Republicans Abroad met with fury over the House and Senate eliminating the foreign exclusion bill that had been in place to equalize the cost of living abroad. We planned a well-measured attack aiming for the 1980 election, and this is what we did:

❀ We learned that the United States counts the number of people who sign into our embassies to get the numbers of American citizens living abroad. A quick vote showed that only one of us at this table had signed the book.

❀ So we devised a questionnaire to be given on a certain day all over the world. One question was, "Did you sign our embassy's guest book?" Hmm. Only 3 percent of those polled had done so.

❀ One of our members was a CPA between jobs and she offered to canvas Great Britain for all of the U.S. citizens living there. And, by the way, registered them to vote. She registered some 150,000 citizens who worked for Ford, the big banks, our military, retirees, etc.

❀ We sent out postcards asking everyone who didn't get a ballot by October 21 to call a line at our lawyer, Joanie Nelson's, office and register the complaint. I manned the lines and thought it must be lunchtime when it was 7:00 P.M.

❀ We spent the evening calling the head of each election district for each complainant. We told them we were suing them in court unless they could get the ballots here in time for folks to vote and return for counting. The election districts had never seen anything like this. When the ballots were counted Senator Goldwater had lost his seat. So they opened the absentee ballots, which then put him in the winning column.

This was war and the representatives and senators sat up and took notice. They reversed their opinion and reinstated the exclusion for Americans living abroad. We heard this the morning after the royal wedding of Charles and Diana at the embassy coffee for Mrs. Reagan. That afternoon our family sailed home on the *QE2,* and so it was five days before we learned the amount of the exclusion.

As a result of this initiative the Republican National Committee asked me to sit on their board. Because I didn't have one hundred dollars for a ticket to Washington—our new house mortgage had escalated from 10 to 18 percent—every month I had to decline. I have always regretted that sacrifice.

In some cases, American politicians out to get the vote could take a lesson or two from other countries. In Ghana and Benin, traders from Indonesia introduced cotton batiks a few centuries ago. Over time, the patterns evolved to suit the local people, their spirituality, and their politics. Present-day politicians commission bolts of batik with their picture on it. The bolts of fabric, or shirts and dresses made of it, are sold in the fabric markets. Steve and I thought this was particularly clever, especially in locations where there were virtually no sites to plaster with posters except a wooden wall constructed solely for that purpose somewhere along the highway. We visited during election time and virtually everyone wore political clothing.

Religion

Because freedom of religion is one of the founding principles of our society, most of us don't know what it feels like to live someplace without that freedom. We might disagree with certain individuals' choices of what religion to practice, or even think the government ought to support our particular religion more. But we simply don't know the fear of government reprisal for practicing our faith as people in other countries do.

When we packed our things to be shipped to Saudi Arabia in 1984, the children were given a big box for anything beyond clothing. There had been a lot of talk about Bibles not being welcome in the kingdom and nothing outwardly Christian, so we all tried to avoid bringing anything religious.

When we opened Beau's box (he was then ten years old) it was a sea of Legos on top of balls for every sport, some favorite trucks and stuffed animals, board games, and on the very bottom his Bible and his prayer book from church school. The censors were obviously challenged by the Legos and passed over emptying it out. For us it meant that we could have a family church service every Friday, staff day off. Our "church" sessions were always inside, and always had a bit of a clandestine feel to them. After all, we were breaking the law just to have the Bible and prayer book, let alone to be worshipping what the Saudi's considered to be a heretical belief system and "singing the songs" as our Saudi fixer, Ali Shmelan, called it.

Afterward we always played bridge and tennis to fortify what was famously known in the family as our children's "shoe box of social skills." (The shoe box comes up throughout this book, since it ended up being a fairly big box!)

Similarly, celebrating Christmas posed a problem for us. In the buildings of various embassies (recognized under international law to be considered part of the home country's soil), we could celebrate Christmas, and those events were great fun. We had the chance to see a slice of how other countries enjoyed the holiday.

In our own home, though, during our stay in Saudi Arabia, we did have a Christmas tree, and I sold Christmas ornaments—stuffed-felt children's story characters so they were hung with care, and on the top was a Saudi man in a thobe and gutra (head gear), which was made as a pot holder. There was a telephone call system where you called several friends to announce something new we should all know about. This worked well when the Euromarche (Saudi shopping center) got their "holiday bushes" in. You had to hurry down through the list because the mutawa (religious police) knew what Christmas trees were and would take them out for burning.

When Ashley and Van came from boarding school for the holidays we would meet in Africa or Europe to celebrate. We celebrated Christmas in Kenya; in Morroco; skiing in Lech for a week; and then up the Nile in Egypt; and in Spain. I wanted the children to worship Christmas in church, which we couldn't do in Saudi Arabia, so we sought places with churches. Some of the most meaningful moments in my life were singing "Silent Night" with three hundred people—in fifty languages.

Other countries posed other challenges to us on the religion front. In Britain, for example, it took us almost a year to find a church with more regular participants than just our own family. The Brits are not overly religious in general, so this was not an enormous surprise, although even I didn't think it would take a year.

In India enormous religious tolerance is a practicality of life, except where they are in jeopardy of losing territories. Here is a partial list of houses of worship in India: Sikh temples, Parsi fire temples, synagogues of the old variety, Church of India (used to be Church of England), Hindu temples, Buddhist temples, mosques, and more. You are most welcome to enter any of them. We learned that in holy sanctuaries it didn't matter how you toured about some of them, but you should remove your shoes and circumnavigate clockwise in places where it did. So if ever in doubt, wherever we are, we take off our shoes and ambulate clockwise, just in case. This is good travel advice.

In the Western Sichuan Province of China, formerly Tibet, our Chinese guide introduced us to his "very good friend," a Tibetan monk, who was to show us around the main temple. Once out of earshot, our guide gave us his version of the truth. The monks were under the thumb of the soldiers/guides, and some of their works were curtailed. We went outside to admire the facade. Alas, our monk asked if we could read Tibetan. We could not, so he translated the innocent-looking stone, which was in fact a litany of Chinese abuses of the Tibetan temples: how many had been plowed under or rearranged, and the usurping of the traditional form of Lama choice, etc. No one seemed at all concerned that the military could read local dialect. Simply not a chance because of lack of interest.

Money

Traveling to other countries can make you reconsider what "wealth" really is, as well as give you new perspective on what people in other cultures appreciate.

The great animal lover, Gerald Durrell, is one of our family's favorite read-out-loud authors. Even when our children were in their teens we read *Rosie is My Relative* aloud at dinnertime. It is the hilarious story of someone inheriting an elephant and having to bring it home across England. One of his many books, *The Bafat Beagles,* takes place in a small kingdom in the Grassfields, in the northwest highlands of Cameroon.

Bafat is a Tikar community ruled by the fon who has fifty-eight wives, although only five are his and the rest were inherited from his father and grandfather. We arrived during visiting hours and I was introduced to Queen Constance, a very capable woman who had delivered the fon his ninth child. Her eldest was a layabout specimen in pink sandals totally spoiled by his father. Just outside the gates of the kingdom was a large display of freshly laundered T-shirts and jeans, blouses, and skirts for sale suspiciously looking like they had arrived in a black bag from Goodwill. "Ace Mechanics," and "Arkansas," the backs read. A basketball shirt from Oakville was another.

The queen had obviously bought her outfit, a black lace cocktail dress and a green sweater, from this stand. Queen Constance and I immediately bonded when I asked her if a queen of Bafat had a nanny. She laughed a diminishing laugh and said, "No, queens in Bafat are very poor. Come. I will show you my house." It was on a corner and had a small, level patch where vegetables would be planted in a few months. It was devoid of furniture beyond a few futons on the floor and a table. She scolded the little children for good measure and then led me on a tour of the kingdom.

We were stopped several times by various men who asked Queen Constance's decision about a certain problem. She dispensed justice quickly. The yellow-and-purple swathed fon (with matching pillbox hat) approached and they had a brusque exchange. It was clear that she was the brains behind the kingdom and the fon needed her help. The village was beautiful with a magnificent, round Spirit House on stilts. The people are animists and Christians together. Jacaranda trees bloomed everywhere. No one came up to us trying to sell me anything. So I asked the queen if she had anything for sale. She did produce a tray of beads and baskets, most of which I bought. Then she disappeared, and I was on my own to find the way out.

This is an ancient holdover government in Cameroon with its elegance sapped. Queens probably never before had power. But the temptation of being called "queen" outweighed the reality of her squalid lifestyle. My feminist tendencies were certainly aroused. But my admiration for the queen was unsparing. The event continues to haunt me.

Before ATMs, travelers relied on travelers' checks. One time we were off on a holiday from London, and I called Steve at the office to remind him to get money. He was just able to get to the teller's cage before they closed for the day, but there were no travelers' checks. When he got home we were all in our bed watching TV. Steve opened his attaché case to rearrange, and Ashley gasped at the geometrically organized stacks of cash. "*Oh Daddy, what have you done?*" It was the official start of the holiday as there were belly laughs all around and Steve could hardly get his breath.

Libraries

I hadn't heard very much about the new public library at Alexandria on the Mediterranean coast of Egypt. But it was unbelievable that one of the seven wonders of the ancient world was being rebuilt in the shape of a huge circular pipe sheared off at a 45-degree angle, wherein are windows lighting each of the stepped-in seven floors. The outside is sheathed in overlapping slate tiles each carved with a written symbol. No message is intended, only the celebration of all forms of writing. It is an astonishingly simplistic building, but so right in its place.

Inside are very few books. Rather, vast computers store the texts of millions of books. A reader enters the library, finds an unoccupied desk and returns to the checkout desk to request specific books. The reader's card accesses the system and the requested books are downloaded onto the terminal at the reader's desk. It is a simple system. Could we not convert every library in the world to this system and never need to shelve books again? A few years later my friend Dane Mellor and his partners created Books on Demand, a machine which prints any book you want in about three minutes, and placed one of three prototypes in the library at Alexandria. The other two were in the World Bank headquarters in Washington, D.C., and at the New York Public Library. The oldest library in the world is still the most relevant.

Perhaps the most unusual library I ever visited was in Bhutan. The people are a bit surly, and I thought resented showing foreigners around. There they make lovely handmade paper not dissimilar to that

Toilet Paper *21*

made in India with violets and small ferns pressed inside. I was able to buy some of that and asked to go to the art college where students displayed their work. I purchased a carved soft wood dagger with an interesting totem handle of fierce animal heads. I asked to see the library and was taken to the National Library that seemed to have no books.

"Where are the books?" I asked

They pointed to what looked like colorfully covered pads of laundry lists sparsely laid out on shelves set at an angle. No one was allowed to pick them up to show me how they worked.

I was beginning to feel it was a mistake to visit Bhutan with so little of their rich society available to be seen. The next morning we were careening down the mountain curves and passed some interesting birds, which when we asked were told they were the national bird. "But that's what I've come to see!" I said. This cut no ice and we were at the bottom in breakneck record time.

My Cairo hostess and her friend Mary both wanted to drive me to St. Catherine's Monastery on the Sinai Peninsula. We packed for a cold overnight in the desert and headed north disappointed not to be able to see the Suez Canal from the road. The route is under the canal, and the monastery is situated at the end of the canyon our hotel is in. It is an all-day trip, the final half through unusual rock mountains looking like giant fingers much as the thirteenth-century artist Duccio portrayed his mountains. St. Catherine's is the oldest monastery in the world never to be invaded. Even Napoleon passed through and left gifts. It is obvious that this monastery is so far from the beaten path that the monks have no interest in life beyond its walls.

High above it is the mountain where Moses was graced with the Ten Commandments. Inside the walls is the burning bush, which is growing into a tree 3,500 years later.

There is a new library there containing icons and illuminated manuscripts of such value that they are comparable to those in the Vatican in rarity. A magnificent church with a spectacular play of sun and light within and monastic cells fill the walled space. We take camels up Moses' mountain, but the preferred way is to climb to the top at 3:30 A.M. in order to see the sunrise.

This is an awesome place. It is an affirmation, a defining moment for an adventurer like me. It is what I live for. Experiencing a place such as this extends the threshold of my patience and calm, and it recharges my battery.

The U.S. Flag

Yes, a cliché, but then, clichés are that way for a reason. When you're traveling and you feel like an island in a sea of new culture, seeing the American flag really is like a guiding beacon. It reminds you that no matter how tough it is that moment, you get to call "home" the greatest country on earth. Billions of people do not get to say that. I feel fortunate. I feel protected. I feel special. The longer I was overseas, the more patriotic I became, even when coming back to the Unites States required its own adjustments.

Ashley's Perspective

It is always a surprise and comfort to stumble across the US Embassy while traveling around the world; I always have a feeling of security when I see our flag. On one occasion, I felt a particular rush of pride finding an American flag at the end of the dirt road while traveling through Laos. Even in the faraway places of the world, the Stars and Stripes reminds us of who we are, where we come from, and that we are never too far away from home. This comfort allows us to discover different cultures and to go even further down that dirt road.

While other countries have palaces, kings, and other historical symbols, Americans have their flag, the only symbol for our country. Perhaps this is why it is proudly displayed on most homes throughout America, a tradition which is not commonplace anywhere else in the world.

Customs/border crossings

Just the process of entering another country also made me appreciate the United States and our freedom even more. Crossing into Saudi Arabia generally meant being seriously groped in nether parts by burly Yemeni women in a back room who apparently were searching for very small, yet very lethal, weapons. Why Yemeni women? The Saudis recruit employees from other countries to do the jobs they felt "beneath" them.

When we moved to Saudi Arabia, I had brought some spices along with kitchen equipment and found some of the tins had various suggested uses blacked out. Pork chops and ham offended the censors as did hamburgers! My art library met with several cautionary episodes. Picasso bosoms, life drawings, and certain Roman sculpture came under attack by the black Magic Marker. In fact I think I am still missing a few books that were just too much for the purist eye. In all of this we never intentionally tried to smuggle in contraband and honestly tried to avoid anything controversial. But of course the suspicious mind knows no bounds.

Cartoons from English Xerox machines mocking the government were in great demand. Tongue-in-cheek letters to the editor hailing off-color TV shows suggesting that they might like to subscribe to, and Olympic divers blanketed in Magic Marker were regular features. We made placemats of the censorships and twenty years later they still fascinate our dinner guests. It was a sad turn of events pushed to the limits by what many expats considered phony or even double-standard morality. Life was hard in the compounds where wives had no cars and small houses, and no one could leave until Dad returned from the office. You wonder why people took these jobs? The pay was a stunning three to five times what they could make at home.

In certain countries just having the passport or visa stamp from a rival country can mean delays. On a joint pilgrimage to Israel with Mother; our Greenwich, Connecticut, church; and the synagogue next door to our church, I experienced a bit of it. It was only two years after the five we lived in Saudi Arabia. My passport was full of visas to Saudi, maybe thirty of them, as we had to apply for permission to leave and a visa to enter. I could see the Israelis were taking a long time with everyone. When we finally got the to front of the line, I said, "Before you even look, let me tell you that I lived in Riyadh for five years, and I knew many Saudi women, my friends even."

They had no trouble finding the numerous visas.

"Why would you want to know them?"

"Because I was living in their country, and they could not leave home. I visited them to keep them company."

Two more questions and Mother (who had two Saudi visas) and I were through the gate.

The plight of women crossing boundaries was understood. They too empathized with the sting of the entrapment and acknowledged it. They honored me by recognizing my humane responsibility.

Another instance of women understanding women came on a recent trip to London. The customs agent seemed highly suspicious of the number of countries we had visited, and continued asking question after question.

CUSTOMS AGENT: How long will you stay?

STEVIE: Three weeks.

CUSTOMS AGENT: Why are you here?

STEVIE: To do family research.

CUSTOMS AGENT: Are you staying with family?

STEVIE: Yes, near the end.

CUSTOMS AGENT: Then why did you write on your entry form that you're staying at the Hilton?

STEVIE: We're staying three nights there and two nights with family.

CUSTOMS AGENT: Where else are you staying?

STEVIE: Hope End in Ledbury and Burts in Melrose.

CUSTOMS AGENT: Have you been here often?

STEVIE: We've lived here on and off for twenty-five years. My husband was running Merrill Lynch International Banking.

CUSTOMS AGENT: Why did you leave?

STEVIE: He was given a job in New York City.

This went on for twenty minutes.

Finally, she asked me "Why are you talking and he isn't?" pointing to Steve. I replied "I know the itinerary and he doesn't."

And then she understood and let us through.

Gifts

All families give gifts, and close families will naturally go to greater lengths to give the perfect gift. This means that close families with a penchant for international living will from time to time go through even greater extremes than most to make sure loved ones have just the right thing.

After three trips to Mexico, I finally got Ashley and Olivier's wedding gifts there that were either too fragile or too large for a suitcase. One day we packed the car in Florida with an Indian bed, cut down to coffee table size, and around it packed wine glasses and framed pictures. We drove to my cousins Robert and Diane in Harlingen, Texas. There we concocted a complicated plot to meet Ashley and Olivier across the border in Nogales.

Robert and Diane led us through customs to the Nogales airport, where we had reserved a rental car for Ashley and Olivier to take the goods. When it appeared as though the right car was not available, Robert put his arm around his new friend, the rental car representative, and told him very pleasantly that he had a lot of friends who came that way who needed to rent cars, but he also had a lot of friends who came that way who liked to burn down houses.

We got the car.

But the table didn't fit.

We gave Ashley and Olivier the wine glasses and pictures, kissed them good-bye, and then drove back in convoy with our cousins to the border, table still in our car.

Robert and Diane cleared immigration easily, but they parked and walked back when it became clear we weren't.

The customs officer took our passports into the office because we had Syrian visas in them. We were interrogated about who we knew in Syria, why we were there, what is there to do for ten days, etc. It was touch and go because 9/11 was still firmly in everyone's memory.

This took close to an hour, and Steve and I were both in suppressed rage mode. We took our car through immigration again, and the very same man who asked about the Syrian stamp stopped us and looked inside, and saw our table.

"Where is that table from? Did you buy it?"

I had a choice of saying it was an Indian bed or what I decided to say. Pointing my agitated index finger I growled, "Don't go there with me!"

He stepped back and waved us through.

Six months later we had a Texas reunion with our cousins who threw the table in the back of their pickup and hauled it to San Miguel de Allende in the colonial section of the country.

Sometimes, I caused the problems myself.

From one of my visits to Ashley in Mexico City, I returned to our farm in the Adirondacks via Montreal. It just happened to be the night of the Blackout of 2003, when the Northeast U.S. grids couldn't meet the demands on a sticky August night. Planes were diverted to places not affected. One of those was Montreal. I got through customs, found Steve, Mother, and Auntie Gray, all of whom had had a wonderful day as tourists, and we headed south to the border.

At the border after midnight, we found a mass exodus with every immigration line open. We inched our way forward and answered the usual questions. Then customs leaned into the car and asked "What did you buy in Mexico?" To which I sleepily replied, "Just a little pot."

"Just a little pot?" he echoed.

"Yeah, a little low-fired ceramic," I replied

"Who's in this car?" he asked, to which I replied, "Just the grannies."

He paused, looked, and waved us through with an angry "Get out of here."

Poor Steve could keep a poker face no longer and pulled to the shoulder gulping with laughter. "He thought you had marijuana!"

Surely the most magnificent entry we witnessed into any country was our walk across the border from Amritsar, India, into Pakistan, near Lahore. When the lines were drawn in 1947 dividing India into two countries, it divided communities and families by two wooden barriers lifted twice a day.

We took a taxi from Amritsar to the border crossing, heavily guarded by the Indian Army on one side and the Pakistani military on the other. The taxi driver told us to stand at the back and side of the forming crowd to watch what was happening. Whole families arrived at both sides, lifting new babies or well-scrubbed toddlers high so to show them off to someone across the border. New brides were introduced to family just caught out by history. There were calls, laughter, and tears in this most uncommon border of reunions.

All went silent and the two armies, precision drill teams, marched and strutted formations and complicated patterns in turn. The flags were lowered at dusk. The barrier went up and the families who could afford the visa fee poured across to greet their relatives on the other side. The others moved down the road to continue their family gossip reaching beseeching arms across the divide. The foreigners were then allowed to cross. I was grateful to the guard for giving us a warning. It's a poignant memory that still puts a lump in my throat.

The Other Side

Appreciation means having renewed enthusiasm for your host country: discovering simple solutions to tricky problems, finding inexpensive substitutes, and revealing yet another delicious way to prepare mangos. I remember showing photos to Greenwich friends of the house we were going to rent in Bombay. They oohed and aahed at the polished wooden sills and floors, but dead silence met the pictures of the kitchen.

"Is *this* how you will live? With a cement tub and an oilcloth-covered table?"

"No, we will add shelves and a stove and fridge and a water purifier in the sink."

"You will live four years like that?"

I hesitated and then quietly said, "I will rarely go into the kitchen, and we want to make a clean and comfortable kitchen for the cook and staff." It was a different world, and difficult to explain that food preparation and clean up are sociable times for the staff, a staff that existed for us overseas because of the different standard of living, the different society, etc. Appreciation meant understanding that we went to other places and accepted them as a package deal.

Appreciation means making sure you don't get caught up focusing on what is "wrong" with a new place and instead looking for what is good.

While in Japan, for example, I could have dwelled on how expensive certain items were, such as the thirty-dollar cantaloupes, but instead I focused on the ready availability of fresh flowers, something that is normally expensive in the United States. The children bought exotic goldfish for pennies. One could buy small portions of food, which was impossible to do then in the United States. There were favorite restaurants that served food on a stick, and you paid by the stick; mouthwatering Osoba restaurants (but don't enter through the parking lot door or Madam won't serve you beer) serving hearty tonkatsu (grilled pork). My favorite was Inakaya, the country-cooking place where a line of cooks sat cross-legged in front of a fire, roasting eggplants, eel, and every manner of food they slipped onto a plate and handed to you on a long-armed paddle.

Although moving around frequently had its downsides, the ability to reinvent myself with every move was an advantage. Each time, I learned better what worked, what didn't, how to make friends quickly, how to spot the people who would be friends (and who wouldn't), and much more. I learned to appreciate the system of support available with the expat circle, and that the advantage of being part of a social circle of expats is that people judge far less. Everyone in the group is at least somewhat out of their element, and with that comes more empathy for others being out of their natural element too. We were each other's aunties, moms, sisters, and daughters.

With the expats not only came understanding, but a practical support system that I very much appreciated as well. We had a system of taking packages home back and forth, as well as picking up odds and ends not easily found in our host country, little luxuries such as stamps, peanut butter, cake mix (the local cakes tasted like fish, which is what they fed cows), and Halloween candy.

The single most important advice I tell young families going abroad for the first time is "never complain." A story can be told many ways but if you moan your way through an episode you'll not get sympathy. Everyone has been there. They will simply run away. Instead, tell a story with irony or with a laugh.

For instance, several of us helped the American Club celebrate the 1976 bicentennial by lending American paintings for an exhibition. To return them someone borrowed a truck and put the paintings in the back so that they bumped their way home. Not surprisingly some damage occurred. One friend arrived home after mah-jongg (Chinese solitaire) and examined the painting still in her front hall. Kiyokosan, her Japanese housekeeper, came out of the kitchen and said, "No worry, Madam. Big problem, but Kiyokosan fix." She held up a Magic Marker! Now, our Barbara dined out on that story for a week. Alternatively, she could have burst into tears, fired the maid, and wept through seven nights of dinner parties never to be invited back.

Other aspects of adapting and appreciating

Adapting to your surroundings goes hand in hand with appreciating them. Sometimes, appreciation comes first, such as in the case of admiring a Japanese garden. This is an easy aspect of Japanese culture to love and admire but difficult to understand, yet the more I learned about the underlying philosophy of their beliefs—always leave one dead leaf in the garden, for example, to show that there is no beauty in imperfection not made by God—the easier it was for me to adapt to their culture.

On the other hand, we had the 3:00 A.M. calls for Steve from his coworkers back in the United States, most of whom seemed to think the entire world functioned on eastern standard time. First, I asked them if they realized it was 3:00 A.M. and did they want me to wake him? Later, I learned to appreciate that they meant well, but I never stopped wishing Steve worked for a firm who called you in your daytime.

Adapting also meant understanding the overall personality of the societies we were in, and finding the good in them. As much as Americans in particular don't like to stereotype—or at least like to pretend we don't—stereotypes are there for a reason. For example, no national image exists of the Australians being shy, although certainly at least one or two must be.

What I found was that different countries had varying degrees of comfort with expressing disagreement, which led to varying degrees of passive-aggressiveness. The Japanese, for example, were, on a whole, very passive-aggressive, which made it challenging to get a straight answer from someone when he or she disagreed with you. Women, for example, would simply giggle when an uncomfortable topic was touched upon, and the polite thing to do was navigate the conversation away from the topic once the giggle was heard.

This created an interesting situation when our Japanese nanny asked me to find her a husband (and in Japanese culture, this was what was done). First, as was the custom, I went to a construction site and called out, "Anyone not married here?" and gave the respondents my calling card so they could arrange a meeting with the nanny.

Our nanny rejected these applicants.

Then I tried taxi drivers.

No luck.

Then a cook.

Still no luck and out of choices, I asked our nanny what I should do. She giggled, and I was off the hook.

The upside to the Japanese culture, though, was that no one yelled. It's nice not to feel like you're doing battle as you drive across town, or if you accidentally do something to offend someone.

The Saudis were on the other end of the spectrum, never afraid to express their feelings openly. There, the upside was that you did not have to guess where you stood. If someone was displeased with you, you knew it, for better or worse. On the other hand, it was a complete act of faith to drive across Riyadh.

Friends at home would ask, "Don't you feel confined by not being able to drive?"

I'd say, "Are you kidding? There are car crashes shoved off the road every quarter mile! I'm perfectly happy sitting in the back with the seat belt securely fastened. Thank you very much!"

By finding aspects of each country to appreciate, I was also trying to focus the family philosophy and outlook on having a positive attitude and not complaining. I learned this the hard way, after having a breakdown when we first arrived in Japan. Everything about Japan was incredibly different or, as we said backward, as in "first you wash and then you get into the bathtub."

Just dealing with the day-to-day aspects of existence with two small children was more than I could deal with. The birth of my youngest son, Beau, was the turning point. He was such a sweet and giggly baby born at ten pounds. He helped turn my outlook around, and I realized that to survive, I had to focus on what was good and adapt to my circumstances. From that point forward, I knew all would be fine, and I learned to appreciate the ability to adapt in myself. I learned to expect the unexpected. While that didn't prepare me for the myriad specific challenges we would continue to face, it did prepare me to be resilient in the face of whatever was happening.

Zen and the Art of Life

It's easier to appreciate your surroundings if you let things happen around you, learn, process, and then act. Learn before you leap. Patience will keep you from making a lot of silly mistakes that you have to clean up after, and keep you from apologizing to your new friends in your new culture. As the saying goes, better to have someone think you are an idiot than open your mouth and prove them correct.

Ashley's Perspective

After moving back from England, when I was entering fourth grade, I felt that part of assimilating into the culture of Greenwich, Connecticut, was copying the local accent. I would practice my American vowels at home in bed before I went to sleep. Mom would hear me say: "I kiant do this," as I tried to mimic my new classmates' accents.

I understood it was a liability to sound different from everyone, and I refused to speak until I got it right. Mom was flabbergasted when my teacher mentioned that I was a quiet student, but I had learned that we must adapt to the local landscape to feel accepted.

Sharing a happy moment.

Patience sometimes requires asking questions over and over until you receive a satisfactory answer. Raising your voice is the most common response to someone who doesn't understand, but if anything, it has the opposite effect.

One day in Tokyo I went out on what I was certain would be a simple mission: purchasing four apples for a lamb curry I was going to make. No matter which market stall I went to, the vendor would not sell me four apples. It made no sense to me, and I kept going from stall to stall in my quest for my four apples. Finally one offered to sell me three, and then pointed to another stall for me to purchase the final apple. It seemed impossible to find out what was going on behind the odd behavior, so I bought the apples in that strange manner.

Finally I found out the explanation. In Japanese, the word for "four" and the word for "death," are the same: "shi." The Japanese will not sell anything in the quantity of four, or even in multiples of four up to the quantity of twenty. Patience was the only way to obtain that answer.

It was also useful in Saudi Arabia when trying to decipher the truth behind stories. After many baffling moments of trying to figure out why the same story told by several different people all were different, I learned that for Saudis, a story properly told meant it wasn't told the same way twice. What I was looking for—consistency and factual evidence—just didn't exist within the framework of the oral tradition in Saudi Arabia. It is bad manners to bore your audience so the elements are changed. It is not considered lying, merely good storytelling.

Naturally there is also the patience required not only by cultural difference, but basic language barriers too. We had a beloved African Gray parrot in Saudi Arabia, and one day the parrot was out of food. I asked our driver, Adam, to "get big bird food," which was different from what our small cockatiels needed.

Several hours later, Adam returned with a frozen turkey—no small feat in Riyadh, where tracking down such a thing is nearly impossible. No small feat, but it made no sense to me.

Seeing the puzzled look on my face, he enthusiastically said, "Big bird food" as he proudly handed the frozen turkey to me.

How you can use this

Although I had a built-in advantage by reinventing myself every time we moved, this is something you can do for yourself, too, anytime you want. You don't even have to move to another continent.

How? Take a look at what is working in your life and what is not. The advantage you have by *not* moving is that you can take one item at a time; you don't have to change everything all at once. You certainly can if you'd like, though!

What's the one thing in your life that you would like to change? What habit or trait is holding you back the most? Every day is a new day, and you can start fresh whenever you'd like.

Be patient with yourself as you change. I learned that most other cultures are far more patient with their children, only yelling at them when a dangerous situation required it. (The Japanese would yell, "Hai, hai, hai" (yes, yes, yes) to a child running toward a moving car. Give the gift of patience to your children, and also to yourself as you change and grow.

Appreciating Art

I found learning about the art in whatever country we were in to be one of the best ways to meet people, get into their culture and to understand the people. The myriad ways people express themselves creatively and what others see fascinates me.

We became big collectors of silk carpets in Saudi—so much so that our dealer and two or three of his handlers would bring them out to our mud palace, where the rooms were 60–100 ft long. The first time the handlers brought in all the carpets, there was one who stood in front of our painting by Frank Faulkner, which was tinted gel swirls and dots and stigmata hands. He stood so reverently that I asked our dealer what it was that the boy saw in the painting. He said he saw himself as a little boy tying the minute carpet knots, with his hands bleeding at the end of each day. I asked the dealer then that he always bring this young man every time he came because he seemed to appreciate it more than anyone else.

In Saudi Arabia, a group of visiting spouses and I found a heart-shaped, white-metal-and-brushed-gold pendant in an antiques shop in Jeddah. Steve, who loves buying jewelry, was very excited when I showed it to him back at the hotel. He and I retraced the day's travels, and I took him back to Mohammed, a pleasant Afghani entrepreneur selling textiles, jewelry, and metal objects from around the Middle East.

Steve interrogated him about the decorative pendant I had bought, and thus was the beginning of a long and wonderful friendship. This was 1985 and the Turkoman tribes were selling their jewelry to buy surface-to-air missiles to shoot down Russians. Steve was as fascinated with the reason for sale as he was the original jewels. As the months passed the quality of the jewelry became finer and more antique.

Mohammed often went to Afghanistan to bring out more goods and stopped in Riyadh to sell to his clients there. Along with the beautiful jewelry several of us bought saddles, riding crops, and other objects offered. Most of the jewelry was for women, but one hat (that must have weighed eight pounds) was a boy's cap covered with rings of Maria Theresa silver coins—the coin of the realm not so long ago. There were gourds decorated with lapis and carnelians used for tobacco.

At one point Mohammed returned with the heavy repositories of a bride's wealth. This was the end of a fatiguing war and they had saved the best for last. Collections of large, silver heart-shaped pendants, detailed in silver filigree and decorated with carnelians, were worn between the bride's braids. There were six-inch decorative buttons and cape clasps, brushed with gold; Koran holders decorated with fringes of metal work and bells weighing more than five pounds each were worn around the neck. There were tall wedding crowns of brushed gold-and-red fabrics, decorated in white metal and stones, and bracelets with up to six courses of repeat designs. Six-inch-wide heart-shaped bangles were made to be worn between the pigtails of a girl and uniquely adorned decor for the narrow waists of the girls. We later found modern bracelets had as many as twelve courses.

Mohammed asked some of us to go with him to Afghanistan. We would ride on donkeys over the mountains from Pakistan. We reluctantly said we thought we would be mistaken for Russians! We didn't make the trip, but the idea still fascinates me.

In Bombay we had Jewish friends whose family legends included one about a young Iraqi bride, dressed in her wedding clothes laden with pounds of Turkoman jewelry, who was placed (in this state you cannot walk unaided) on a mounting block to wait for Dad who had just gone to bring around the camel. Meanwhile, a young fellow passing on horseback spotted her, galloped across barely slowing down to sweep her up into his arms. She never saw her family again. They point out it didn't make much difference as she had never seen the intended husband and he wasn't her choice anyway. She was our friend's great grandmother.

In London we inquired at the British Museum if they would like to see our collection of Turkoman jewelry, which they did, and which no doubt they were hoping we would give them as their few pieces were poor examples. Interestingly, they didn't want to show our collection unless they owned it.

Later in Greenwich, Connecticut, the collection was mounted in an exhibition at the Bruce Museum as a curiosity. Loved by many, some thought it too primitive for the new image of the Bruce they were trying to cultivate. In Florida we display them on a platinum and silk tree-of-life carpet with five hundred knots to the square inch in the open, spotlighted fireplace (so unnecessary in the subtropics).

Turkoman jewelry found its way to other countries too. In St. Petersburg, Russia, I followed my nose to a gallery separated off by a velvet curtain, which swished aside just as I was passing, where I got a glimpse of their fabulous collection, including the spoils of war: belts and horse gear. They also had many beautiful pieces of Turkoman jewelry that they didn't want the general public to see, perhaps because it had been brought back from the war? I asked to see their collection in storage and was told each drawer I wanted to see would cost me one hundred dollars!

Stevie and Jaxon, her oldest grandchild, sharing a moment, Casey Key, 2006.

Steve and Stevie, 2006.

How you can use this

No matter how challenging the situation there is redeeming value to be found, even if it takes time and energy to unearth it. Finding it and focusing on it, though, is well worth the trouble. You'll experience less stress and more happiness when you find things to appreciate. How to do that? Say you're stuck on a runway in an airplane in the middle of winter, not taking off and not being let off the plane. The bathrooms are backing up. You have a small child in the seat behind you, using your seat as a soccer ball. Pretty awful, right? What *is* there to appreciate?

Well, at least you didn't try to take off in bad weather and end up sliding off the runway (or worse). With any luck you have a good book, noise-canceling headphones, and backup batteries for those headphones, right? (You *do* travel with those items, or will start immediately, correct?) When was the last time you had the gift of stillness for several hours?

Yes, it's better to choose when you have that stillness. But the point is to make the best of any situation by finding the good in it. Find more good, complain less.

Robert R. Spaulding, Stevie's father, Europe, 1944.

THREE

R-E-S-P-E-C-T

Respect for ourselves guides our morals.
Respect for others guides our manners.

—Laurence Sterne

Respect for right conduct is felt by everybody.

—Jane Austen

We must build a new world, a far better world—
one in which the eternal dignity of man is respected.

—Harry S. Truman

The word "respect" has a spectrum of meanings. On one end of the "respectrum" is the more personal and passionate, "He earned my respect," meaning admiration or a measure of esteem. Without behaving respectably, you "don't get no respect" as Rodney Dangerfield would say. I'm quoting him, but I don't like him very much. On the other end of the respectrum is the cooler, more intellectual principle that Harry Truman offered when he said, "We must build a new world, a far better world—one in which the eternal dignity of man is respected"—that we all inherently deserve to be treated respectfully, with courtesy, no matter who we are and no matter what the surrounding circumstances may be. As I see it, the respectrum spans the distance between treating a person with courtesy and having deep respect for a person.

The objects of my respect fall nicely upon the respectrum. Moving from the more courteous to the more heartfelt, we have: respecting other cultures and other ways of life (abstract, polite, and courteous), respecting my country (abstract, heartfelt, and personal), respecting others in my family and my friends (deeply personal and heartfelt), and respecting myself (the core of all respect for others).

Respect for others comes easily when we're in familiar territory, when people are behaving in a way that we would. Encountering the unfamiliar, though, challenges our ability not only to act with courtesy, but to admire something deeper about the unfamiliar way of life. I have taught my children that acting with courtesy in these circumstances is a key component in their shoe box of social skills. Without our courtesy, others will think we have disdain for them and they will avoid us.

With practice, treating people with ready courtesy becomes the ability to find and appreciate the common ground we share with them. Once you start out treating people with courtesy, it is amazing how often people will recognize and reciprocate it.

On the other hand, if you are the one hoping to acquire respect, knowing that you must *earn* it is also a valuable part of your shoe box. In other words, give basic courtesy freely, and always act from the position that you must earn respect.

There are many points along the respectrum. I think that respect is probably the most important ingredient in any shoe box of social skills, and I learned over time that getting to respect another culture has several stages. First is the basic courtesy we offer and hope to receive that begins at initial contact. As I gained experience traveling and living abroad I was able to program myself for the unexpected, which made the "holy shit" factor a lot easier to cope with. Second, I cautiously give my new surrounds leeway from the "acting respectfully" end of the respectrum, but I am hoping to meet local people with whom I can connect.

Third, as new friendships grow, it becomes easier to be courteous in a locally familiar way and, as a result, my curiosity and understanding grow. I think it's important to say that during this experience, I really wrestle with how the new and different context can work with the greater scheme of my beliefs, ideals, and outlook. Last, I take stock of my life and see that my interactions have moved along the respectrum, from acting with courtesy toward really appreciating what a culture can offer. For any number of reasons, though, a person can be held up at any stage of this process and end up unable to find a real sense of heartfelt respect. This generally doesn't happen to me. I keep looking.

Behaving respectfully, though, does not mean embracing another's way of life. All that is really required is common courtesy and an understanding that there *is* a difference. Different can just be *different,* and accepting differences can mean traveling through life with a lot less to worry about. As Beau likes to say, "Behaving respectfully feels good. You can let yourself off the hook for not knowing everything."

Saudi Arabia

Detached: Thanks, but no thanks

Saudi Arabia was easily the most repressive culture that we lived in. It was a huge adjustment for the entire family, but we found plenty of ways to be happy there. With that said, fear is a powerful saboteur of happiness. I regularly battled away (battling includes, but is not limited to, laughing, researching, reasoning, discussing, and sharing) the fears that others would try to instill in us as we ventured to a new country.

A good example of this was Steve's first right-hand man in Saudi Arabia, Ali, who provided a particularly good test of my ability to battle unjustified fears. A Saudi, Ali lectured me every day about the problems I would have in his country. He was trying to instill in me a respect for his culture by making me afraid. Many of his warnings were real and useful; others were expressed only to intimidate me.

Receiving, but not wanting, his input wore me down. He had to go. I was much happier when we agreed that Ali would have a desk at work and not make my library his headquarters. There were plenty of other people who could be a resource to me without being threatening. One of them, however, was not the emir of Dir'aiyah.

Diplomacy, the old-fashioned way

Occasionally I would be in the pool when the emir came into the garden on a mission. One of the male staff was always within earshot and able to guide him out a side door and around to the vegetable garden or other destination. He never understood that he wasn't allowed in our family garden without permission.

One day I returned from a writing visit to the ruins across the street, and there was a little workman planting dozens and dozens of lime trees in our family garden. I went berserk, rushing around the garden pulling up the sprigs, throwing them over the wall, and slandering the gardener for trespass. Our Ethiopian cook, Milky, came running with all the staff. "Madam, Madam, let us help, please come into the house," they gently persuaded.

I said, "Milky, bring me the garden shears."

"Oh no, Madam. Please let us handle this."

"Milky, this is the last time this will happen."

He got the shears, and I trudged up the hill to the emir's new compound: four palaces, one for each wife. Milky was huffing and puffing behind, but I sent him home because what I had to do would not be a success if there were an Arabic speaker with me.

At the emir's gate, I greeted "good mornings" in English, and walked to the first flower bed in the gardens in front of the administrative palace. I cut every flower head off and moved to the next doing the same, being careful not to touch, let alone pick up a severed head as it could be considered stealing.

Men flew out of the administration building waving their arms and yelling in Arabic. I turned and bowed and said charming "good mornings" and went back to work. They could not speak English, but more importantly, they could not touch a woman.

I happily completed one side of the courtyard when I saw—to my alarm—a lime tree! I went to work on that, and when I was done there was only one leaf left on that bald sucker. Along the third side I made short work of the flowers and looked over at the guard house where the guard was hurrying over to me.

"What you do? What you do?" he screamed.

I smiled brightly, "The emir helps me with my garden, so I help him with his."

There was my driver, Adam, a Somali weight lifter, leaning against the guard house, with his thick arms crossed over his broad chest and a sneer on his face. Glory, I thought, we'd better get out of here.

"Hello, Adam," I said.

"Hello, Madam," he responded.

We walked to the big, navy blue Mercedes full of my four male staff who had driven up the hill as my army. Adam handed me into the backseat and carefully placed the shears in the trunk. As he got in the guard pointed his thumb at me and asked Adam, "Who is this person?"

"That," said Adam, "is my boss."

He closed the door, turned the car around and we proceeded slowly down the hill to our mud house compound three hundred yards away with an audience of well over one hundred people staring from the emir's compound.

Later that day the emir issued an informal statement that he didn't know who had been in his garden. Our ambassador could only say, "Oh Stevie!" when I saw him at drinks that evening. But the British Ambassador actually gave a formal toast to me and "my successful retaliation." Sir Stephen was famous for hating the man he forever called, "Stevie's Emir!" And Sir Stephen was forever my hero for embracing my antagonized arrogance. The emir never came into the family garden again.

I'd like to point out that the tactic I used to get the emir to respect our space was the same tactic that Ali tried to apply to me. It seems clear that in the Saudi culture, fear is a tool that earns you respect.

Beau's Perspective

Dir'aiyah was a wonderland for a fifth grader like me. It was a working date-and-lemon farm, situated in an oasis. I was left to myself to build Lego space stations in irrigation ditches, trap bugs in jars, and explore the ruins across the wadi (dry riverbed) from our house. Our house was palatial, with extra rooms and enormous entertainment spaces. Our bedrooms were off of a walled-in roof, which acted as an excellent courtyard for skateboarding, soccer, and mischief. In the summer, it got as hot as 140 degrees Fahrenheit in the shade. My parents buffered us from that, taking us to other places during the heat.

The parties Mom and Dad threw out on that rooftop were legendary: candles, wine, starlight. Mom had a way of making things look just right, and she laid truly beautiful tables.

The house in Riyadh, which we later moved to, was a true palace. It was a marble villa, designed for a niece of the king. There were countless bathrooms, every amenity, and plenty of rooms for the staff. We moved there because the emir wanted Mom out of his hair. I love her for that. I keep thinking about him thinking of my Mom, saying to himself, "That was one crazy broad . . ."

The Riyadh house was new. It had no quirky smells and everything worked well. Honestly it was pretty antiseptic when compared with the dusty oasis of Dir'aiyah.

Arabs would drag race their brand new Mercedes/Ferraris/Maseratis up and down our street. It was ideal for them: a mile long, straight as an arrow, and in town.

The house was close enough to a commercial area that I could ride my skateboard to get a shawarma, a CD, or an Ocean Pacific T-shirt. That was cool. The best thing about moving to town was that we were so much closer to the bustle of the city. I had more independence: I rode my skateboard to French lessons a half-mile away, and I could practice skateboarding on the smooth, newly paved roads surrounding the villa. I could go to friends' houses nearby.

Mom and Dad had friends over all the time to play tennis. I was a useful guy to have around, if they needed a fourth. Mom entertained like crazy out of that house, and parties were the norm. Downtime was a treat. Getting my parents to myself was a real gift. Sometimes, the most normal times we would know during a year would be in transit, in a hotel, or on a train going somewhere. There, at least, we were all together, and weren't expecting people over for lunch, tea, dinner, tennis, cocktails.

Role reversal

I would be lying if I said all differences were created equal and equally easy to accept. They aren't. I struggled with the religious mandates of tradition and law in Saudi Arabia, particularly those rules that, in my mind, subjugated women. To my view, women were publicly treated like spoiled children: responsible for nothing, accountable to no one, disregarded as useless and utterly coddled. Privately, though, wives held an important role as mistresses of their own homes and keepers of the money, but they were neither given, nor expected, any right to participate in the world outside their gates. They were treated like royalty, as long as they didn't leave their homes. Outside their homes, they were "protected" like children, in effect making them second-class spectators to a society run by the men they married and the boys they raised. All this was challenging for my mind to accept, as women *didn't even have a place* in the public world.

After we had moved into the city of Riyadh, a good Saudi friend of mine, who was a gifted artisan and quite westernized by years of exposure to both the United States and Europe, found herself in a cultural bind that tested my respect for Saudi culture. In many ways she was like me. She had houses in the United States and in Europe and fancy cars in both places, and she enjoyed the freedom and independence that I relish: simple things like driving the children, shopping, and meeting friends for lunch.

But this couple was Saudi, and when they were in Riyadh, she never complained about her confinement. Her husband had a justifiably terrible reputation for drinking, drugs, and women when he was out of the country. One night he indulged himself too much and died in a hotel.

I called on my friend to give her my condolences and a gift of assorted filled dates, and surprisingly I was the only one there at that time. Normally anywhere from three to fifteen friends would be visiting after a tragedy like that.

This intimate setting gave me an opportunity to learn what was on her mind. She offered me one of the dates and conveyed to me that she was now on new footing with her eldest son, the new head of the family. "He will be the one now, at age thirteen, to decide if he should give up smoking, get a cut in allowance, or determine where and when we go on holiday," she said.

She was sitting there in the half-light, trying to remember if she had reprimanded him and for what. What will he hold against me? Is there any reason he might be vindictive? Knowing the wisdom of thirteen-year-old boys, I was struck with grief for my friend. Her status had fallen so far: from international jet-set mom to homebound Saudi crone. Still, she knew how her situation would be different in the West, and she chose to play a traditional role and remain in Saudi Arabia. I liked her. I *respected* her.

As much as she and I were alike, I have rarely felt so cognizant of the cultural divide between a friend and myself as I did in that moment. Each of us is bound to our upbringings in inexplicable ways. What kind of person am I if I judge this person? A judgmental one, and *my* religion clearly warns me not to do that.

The line between child and adult, and the proper treatment of each in Saudi Arabia was a source of anxiety for me throughout our stay. Cooler heads prevailed, though, in rough patches.

For example, there was the day Steve was stopped with twelve-year-old Ashley riding in the front seat. "Why is your wife in the front seat?" the officer asked.

Seriously?

The notion that a man in his forties would have a preteen wife was perfectly acceptable to the Saudi policeman.

Unfazed, Steve proceeded to mime as best he could their father-daughter relationship, including rocking his arms while holding an imaginary baby and pointing to Ashley at the same time. Steve's pantomime skills were tested that day. Ashley, twelve years old, had quite an impression from all this. I wasn't sure at the time if she was more amused or terrified by the whole incident. Now I know exactly how she felt.

Ashley's Perspective

As a young adolescent trying to grapple with all of life's changes and living in an utterly unfamiliar place, I spent a lot of time feeling vulnerable and afraid. On that particular day, Dad and I were driving, as I was to perform on stage with the school band at the International School. It would have been a natural, American moment if it had been in the United States. Instead, I realized that the cop thought I was my father's mistress. He looked at me like I was some kind of object. It was truly frightening. Dad later told me he considered trying to outrun the cop, as he wasn't sure what was going to happen. An average American girl doesn't face this kind of vulnerability and scrutiny. It has made me like Mom: tough as nails.

One Christmas, Steve was meeting Ashley at the airport, where she was arriving to spend the holiday with us. Only fourteen years old, the airport personnel found it reasonable to detain her and the children of other expats after they landed. Steve and other concerned parents stood on the other side of the customs barrier, anxious about the well-being of their children. Finally, as officials subjected Ashley to a lengthy interrogation, Steve jumped the barrier to be with her, eventually gaining her release to join the family as originally planned. This is an important lesson. We all have a point at which we, each in our own way, jump the barrier—a point at which we simply cannot respect an unfamiliar system. Even if we are somewhere new, we must not forget where we come from. From time to time, we have to jump the barrier and do what would be right by the rules that we live by, in the places we come from.

Interestingly, I had an opportunity to share the story of Steve jumping the barrier with the Saudi Minister of Culture. He flatly denied that Ashley had been treated in the way I described. He called me a liar, telling me that, "God looks at you and weeps." I somehow miraculously kept quiet and sought out a different table to dine that evening rather than sit by him.

I would like to think, though, that I dealt with these issues gracefully, at least as far as my children were concerned. I tried to share my views from the standpoint of what we believed in, not what was "wrong with them." Of course, the Saudis did have their flexibility, too. For example, the loud speaker of the mosque used to announce the calls to prayer five times dailywas ten feet from our bedroom. When we told them that we were all Christians, they moved the bell ten feet further away from the wall. From where we lived, we could hear the bells of eight mosques. I think perhaps even *they* thought that was enough.

I also tried to teach my children to deal graciously with the little idiosyncrasies of different cultures and people that really have no explanation and simply trigger a curiosity response. For example, in India many locals seemed to like to be complimented (and this proved true whether Hindu, Muslim, Sikh, Farsi, Buddhist, or other). We are all familiar with the typical Western restaurant maitre d' inquiring if all is satisfactory. That happened there too, but with an eagerness of anticipation that told you they were just about to burst with pride and couldn't wait to hear the magic words—"delicious and beautiful."

It was not just in restaurants, either. It seemed as though every service had a printed questionnaire, every visitors' book had a remarks column, accompanied by someone cheerfully checking to ensure you completed it thoroughly. "Oops, Madam, you left this blank," or "Oh, just a little more room on the bottom line to add your thoughts." This sort of social trait is so easy to engage gracefully. It is engaging people along this sort of line that makes really loving a place so much easier to do. You start with courtesy, you find a way to understand, and, sometimes, you end up caring deeply.

Family, Island Nations, and Xenophobia

As much as many of the differences were difficult for me to fathom, the children did well, not just in Saudi Arabia, but throughout our travels. Most children start out with the innate ability to accept differences without question; it's only after they hear us talk about so-and-so's hair, car, body weight, clothing, etc., that they learn to recognize differences and judge based on those differences. In comes judgment and out goes the "inherent respect" end of the respectrum.

In that sense, our ongoing moves around the globe helped our children immensely. They didn't know that anything was different because they didn't have anything ordinary and regular on which to judge their surroundings. Things just were, and that was one of the gifts to them of our lifestyle. With constant change came a ready acceptance of other people and places.

As with Steve and me, some of the children's acceptance came from the close relationships they developed with each new array of people who helped make our lives possible overseas. Although nannies are a luxury in the United States, they are much more common overseas for various reasons having to do with a lower expense, the reality of life, and the increased difficulty in getting everyday errands done, especially with frequent work-related entertainment obligations. The children were quite taken with their Japanese nanny, for example, and leaving her was quite traumatic for all of them. In Saudi Arabia, although they were too old for a nanny per se, our other staff members were around and active in their lives. Their early one-on-one experiences with different people from around the world (Japan, the Philippines, Ethiopia, and Somalia, to name a few), people who in a very basic sense helped them survive, made them largely unaware of different skin colors and race.

Of course, the children's experiences abroad also gave them a good sense of what it felt like to be the one who was not respected because of nationality, skin color, and so forth. Xenophobic island nations such as Japan and Britain seem to specialize in ensuring foreigners feel out of place, so while we were busy trying to understand others, they were sometimes looking askance at us for being in their country and for being different. This was a common and persistent challenge to seeking a positive relationship with a new place: we know that courtesy begets courtesy, but it is certainly not always the case, and for children, that can be a painful lesson.

What I thought I had discovered about island nations ended up being true about all nations, or, more accurately, just people in general. I think that all people are xenophobic to some degree. According to my dictionary, xenophobia is a "fear or contempt for that which is foreign, especially for strangers or foreign peoples." When we lived in Japan, we found it to be very welcoming on some levels, but very xenophobic on others. The international community that we knew in Tokyo was very welcoming. One of my best friends in the world to this day was an English neighbor of ours in Tokyo. We had some wonderful Japanese friends, but on the whole, local Japanese didn't appreciate us as much, and I assumed it was at least in part because Japan has had such an insular culture and history and because it is an island nation.

There is the example of my friend Mrs. Maki, who was a dynamic force in getting foreign and Japanese women together in friendship after World War II. She told me the tale of her childhood. She was raised in San Francisco where the Americans thought her manners very stylized, novel, and downright peculiar: taking off her shoes at the door and bowing to elders was so very Japanese! Sometimes Mrs. Maki traveled with her family to Japan where they thought her manners were barbaric: she didn't count with the correct fingers and didn't know not to sit in the display area of the main room; thus they deplored her American manners. She didn't fit in either place. Frankly, she was an early visionary and model for what so many people are trying to do today, which is to bring different people and ideas together, to make the world smaller.

Having said this, there were many joys to be found in the Japanese way of life. Some speed bumps felt like high jumps, but they got easier to handle with time. England offered us similar challenges, but most of those, too, could be laughed off and enjoyed with the right perspective.

The Brits, for all their seriousness and stiff upper lip, have as many silly laws as anyone else. We lived in Britain in 1976, during a major drought, and learned we needed a permit to use a garden hose (a "flex"). Dutiful temporary resident that I was, I went in search of the appropriate permit.

The first logical stop seemed to be a garden store, and I brought our garden hose with me. The store clerk looked askance at the hose, and at me. "Are you running that thing without a permit?"

He directed me to the post office to obtain a permit. After the store clerk's reaction to my flex, I knew exactly how to answer when the postal worker asked if I'd been using the hose.

"Absolutely not. Wouldn't dream of it."

I received the appropriate license for the size, shape, and color of my flex and went merrily on my way. Easily finding my way through that kind of bureaucracy earned me the admiration of a few of my British friends.

Some challenges couldn't be laughed off, though. Van caught the brunt of anti-American sentiment at his school in London.

Van's Perspective

I was seven or eight when I went to the St. Barnabas & St. Philip's School for boys in London. On the first day of school, at recess, I was cornered by a bunch of my classmates. Jason, the toughest kid, was sent in to bully me. "Give him the windmill, Jason!" I ducked a swing and punched him right in the gut. Jason fell to the ground with a grunt that was audible because of the shocked silence of the group.

The leader of the group, Charles, put his arm around me and from that moment on he became my good chum. I still got into a lot of fights, but I won most of them. The school thought that I could take care of myself, and Mom had to come to school a number of times to collect me, finding various class-mates of mine with bloody noses and split lips. I think my classmates were so anti-American in part because it was a tough economic time for England, in part because England had fallen so far in stature in the world, and in part because England is an island nation. I also think that fear and suspicion of out-siders are human traits, and are not so easily overcome.

Political Correctness is a Gentle Form of Xenophobia

The door to a discussion on political correctness is now open, or at least cracked, so I will walk through it and discuss our peculiar Amer-ican trait. Political correctness is not something people in most other places give much thought to. In much of the world outside of the United States, if you are treated differently because of skin color, race, religion, or any other of myriad defining characteristics, it is your problem to figure out how to deal with it. The majority is the major-ity for a reason, after all. For the majority group in most countries, it can be really difficult to earn respect if you are different. In the United States, a measure of courtesy is given to all. While this fits within the American set of ideals, it sometimes has the effect of glossing over those aspects of a person's background that individuate them. On a larger scale, the glossing over of peoples' individuality can create cul-tural xenophobia, saying, in essence, "It doesn't matter where you are from, you are *here* now."

Does the notion of political correctness make us Americans crazy? Not any more than anyone else. Overzealous? No. Codependent on a mass scale? Perhaps. Have we turned basic respect for others on its head? No. Does political correctness and the concern for those who are not in a position of power to speak for themselves reflect a good side of our country, part of the ideals upon which we were founded? Yes. In the United States we to tend to specialize in making sure the underdog has his or her day. One of the ways we manifest this is by offering respect freely to all, or at least paying lip service to doing so. When it comes to adapting, should a minority culture have to adapt to the majority? Yes it should. Should the majority make concessions to help the minority culture along? Yes it should.

Political correctness is, at its heart, a noble idea. As is the case with most things, anything good can be taken to extremes, and perhaps we do so with inclusiveness, just as some other countries do with a cavalier, "who cares?" attitude about anyone in the minority. Political correctness is a sort of American-mandated courtesy. Courtesy, or respectful behavior, should not *have* to be mandated. In our country, it is, perhaps in the high hope that by using respectful words we will find deep and abiding respect in our hearts for others.

As you probably suspect from the paragraphs above, I have great respect for our country. Balancing this respect with the realities of being overseas can be challenging. Time and again we saw expats from one nation or another insist that the country they were in should feel, sound, and smell like their homeland. A great example of this was an American woman during my early days in Japan. "Why don't they learn from us Americans how to do things right? There are so many of us here!" This comment came from a woman who, infuriated by a lack of mail delivery due to a postal strike, barged into a Tokyo post office and began ransacking the mail to find hers. I don't understand how that behavior isn't obnoxious in any culture. But I cannot emphasize enough that, contrary to popular American belief, it is not just the boorish "Ugly American" visitor who does this. Boorish tourists come in every size and shape and nationality. Indeed, even the French can be, although it would be a rare day indeed to hear one of them admit it.

You can love your own country and enjoy what another country has to offer. Even if you can't find a heartfelt respect for the nation you are visiting, common sense indicates that beating your head against the wall, trying to change what you cannot, is futile. And aggravating. If we want everything to be like our own backyard, there's really no sense in going anyplace else, right? The precise reason we've always traveled has been to experience new things.

With the security that you can love your own country and enjoy the one you're in comes the ability to embrace local holidays and events that you simply won't get to experience anyplace else. The Indian festival of Ganesh Chaturthi is that way. Guy Fawkes Day in Great Britain is that way. There are a million local opportunities to enjoy celebrations in other places. Skipping them because they are not like home is truly a criminal form of willful ignorance. Again, those festivals are big reasons why people like me travel: to get out and see new things.

Beau's Perspective

In the United States, by insisting upon language that is totally inclusive, courtesy is required, but heartfelt respect for a foreign (read: new) folkway, more, or social pattern is glossed over and essentially denied. In this way, our American society is xenophobic to the degree that it is politically correct. It's not just island nations: all cultures have varying degrees of xenophobic tendency.

For me and probably for Van and Ashley as well, cultural identity was a huge struggle as a child. The fear of being denied social equality in my social environments: school, birthday parties, church, the park, etc., was overarching. It was tough as Americans in London, but it was downright brutal coming from London and living in the United States. After all, we had English accents, and the American kids noticed.

Cultural xenophobia can't really be proved anywhere, but folks who live internationally as outsiders or expats feel its presence in almost everything they do. As an international family, coming to the United States was as foreign as going to Saudi Arabia. I had hoped to find *home.* What I found was more people, living differently, afraid of outsiders, unwilling to compromise on what they knew.

Steve's Perspective

Vietnam, thirty years later . . .

Stevie and I were both quite excited to get to Vietnam, as it is a distinct Asian culture, and I had left Saigon in December 1968 after a tumultuous year. We banked in under the low-hanging rain clouds and saw the rich greens and browns of rice-field paddies surrounding the Hanoi Airport. In March 1968 we had heard rumors that we (the 101st Airborne Division) were going to parachute in and take the airport as part of a full-scale invasion of the North. As pathfinder officer of the 101st Airborne, I would have been the first man out the door. I'm glad we didn't do it.

In our thirtieth anniversary visit, the customs and immigration people wore the same uniforms as the North Vietnamese Army (NVA) had many years before, and it made me slightly nervous, but we put up with a bit of arrogance and kept a low profile. I am a soldier, and one soldier always knows another.

The countryside was spectacularly beautiful, particularly Ha Long Bay with its limestone stalagmites projecting up out of the water, straight up for hundreds of feet. Hanoi was a lovely old French provincial town with broad streets, grand boulevards really, lined with ancient plane and chestnut trees, and the old colonial administrative buildings looking very Greek Revival. But there was a colorlessness about the city. The tourists were the only ones wearing bright clothes, and locals did not approach you. We had the sense of people watching us all the time.

We were particularly fascinated with the sense of humor that revealed itself in the water puppets. Dragons and fish and people caricatures were manipulated on long poles around a pond within a theater. The manipulators were dressed in black, so like the Kabuki theater in Japan, they were meant to be invisible. Occasionally a dragon would rise in his hind quarters and spray the audience, particularly amusing the children. There was a story line that I didn't quite get, but I'm confident good triumphed over evil.

The food was exceptionally good, a cross between Chinese and French cuisine.

We flew from Hanoi down to Hue, the ancient capital near the center of the country and spent a couple of days in and around the center of the old city. The ancient citadel was a museum showing—in good Communist form—the decadence of the old Bao Dai regime (emperor until 1949) and the glories of modern socialism. We found the spot on the ramparts of the Citadel where, in 1968, we would land one helicopter and liaise with the Vietnamese units to prepare for major air assaults by helicopter out into the A Shau Valley. Many days I left here in the first of a fleet of helicopters, expecting not to make it back. This valley was the supply pipeline down which the NVA funneled food and weapons to the Vietcong guerillas and NVA regulars down in the South around Saigon, now "Ho Chi Minh City." In the Tet offensive in 1968, the NVA had overrun Hue, but after weeks of fighting, the NVA were annihilated by the 5th Marines and the 101st Airborne. The city and the citadel still bore the scars.

In 1998 on our way to the Hue airport to fly south to Da Nang, we passed the gates of a military base and I recognized it as the base camp of the 101st, albeit with new slogans painted everywhere. I got our driver to stop and tried to find someone who remembered the old days with the 101st "Screaming Eagles." The driver wandered off and came back with a stooped little old lady who was not afraid to speak her mind. She referred to the NVA as the (string of expletives deleted) VC. Clearly they weren't her national army. We squatted in the dirt for a while and chatted about old times.

We had to check in for our flight early, so we said good-bye and went to the airport. In fifteen minutes she arrived there on the back of a motorcycle, together with a photograph album. We resumed our traditional Vietnamese positions of "hunkering down," squatting in the dirt, and chatted on. She had been a "hooch maid," a daily cleaner who came in to make beds and do laundry for a marine helicopter pilot, a major who flew medical evacuation flights. She bore him two children, cute little girls whose pictures she showed us. He was going to take her home with him and had initiated the paperwork, but a week before he was due to return to the States from his second yearlong tour, he was shot down out in the A Shau Valley. MEDEVAC flights were unarmed and were protected by the Geneva Convention, but Asia only honors such conventions when it appears to be in their interests. He died and her world came to an end. There were many stories like this, and hers rang absolutely true. She was an old warrior, too. Our flight was called and we had to go, but we left her with a fifty-dollar bill, to help take care of her family.

We saw many other interesting sights. Near Da Nang we wandered the ruins of a Champa city, which had had a population of thirty thousand several hundred years before. It was an Indo-based society and the temples had carved images of the Hindu gods, as did Angkor Watt over in Cambodia. The Champa had been exterminated by the relentless pressure of the dominant race in that area. The Vietnamese were also under constant pressure from the Chinese, perhaps making them less tolerant of any possible disloyal pockets in their own country.

The hustle and bustle of Ho Chi Minh City was so energetic and the mercantile activity so strong, that we know that the cold and somber bureaucrats of the North had no chance of controlling them in the long run. In the end, we knew the vibrancy of the South would dominate the North.

The beauty of the country and its culture impressed us greatly, but the most impressive aspect was the strength of one little, old hooch lady who would never surrender her dignity.

Respect for Family Members

Respect within our family was imperative, since we often felt as though we had just each other. The flow of respect from children to parents is considered the given order of things, at least in the early years. The respect from parent to child, though, can be a bit challenging, and I will be the first to admit that. A lingering aspect of giving birth seems to be making our children never experience pain, discomfort, or disappointment. And deciding when to protect them versus when to give them the respect inherently due to them as individuals is particularly challenging when they are not acting respectably.

Where do children land on the respectrum? We love them dearly: we watched them as babies and know their natures better than we know our own, and so we have a deep and abiding respect for who they are. However, when they aren't acting respectably, they show us, as parents, that they aren't able to muster the basic courtesy required to function out in the world. This creates a conundrum!

Sometimes freely giving your children respect, unearned, in the short term helps them earn it in the long term. In other words, sometimes you have to let your children make a decision to crash and burn if it helps them learn. Ashley was a good example of that in the fifth grade. We were living in Connecticut, and she decided to drop out of her previously beloved choir and to stop taking ballet lessons, too, because she didn't like the people. Understanding and respecting my daughter—especially what she could be in the long term—meant acknowledging to myself that I could do nothing to convince her to remain with these activities. She was unreachable at that point. So we spent fifth grade focusing on tennis and hockey, her other favorite activities.

Ashley was unhappy.

At the end of the year, she finally vocalized that unhappiness to me. I asked her, gently, if she thought her current state of affairs had anything to do with her decision to quit choir and ballet. She said she thought it did, and the following year, she rejoined. I don't believe, though, she would have reached that conclusion had I done what was incredibly tempting to do at the beginning of the school year: insist she stay in her room until she changed her mind or turned eighteen. By not forcing her into a situation that I thought would make her happy, I was able to watch her arrive naturally at that happy place on her own.

Van's Perspective

I was at home and completely unenthusiastic about returning to school for my final year of undergraduate studies. I told my mother that retuning to school was completely uninspiring. My mother grabbed a copy of the school's offerings of courses and said, "Let's see what we can find that's fun!" At the end of our discussion, we had picked fencing, counterinsurgency, the history of the opera, and other courses that I actually thought looked like fun.

I felt as if a huge weight had been lifted from my shoulders. Mom turned to me and said, "This school book (the Course Offering) stays at my desk, and if you lose it, you're dead meat!" She then took a black marker and wrote across the front of the book in large letters, "Dead Meat!!" which she then underlined. We both laughed.

Mom knows us: she knows what approach to use and can tell when helping us actually helps.

Beau's Perspective

Mom has always had sympathy for people in tough or desperate situations, and works hard to do something for those who suffer. She has shown us the red-light districts of several world cities, pointing out the ironies of the men, who acted like they were at a carnival, and the women, who seemed to be totally numb and blinded to the bustle of the street. This was particularly sad in Mumbai, where half of the prostitutes were sixteen or younger. It didn't stop there. We would go to the thieves' bazaars, the old markets, the roughest slums in town. She was bold, unafraid, tireless. She demanded a bargain, and had no problem walking away from something she seemed to need. Mom has shown us the seedy underbelly of more cities than I thought had underbellies. She doesn't fear, she doesn't judge, she doesn't question. It just was, and she wanted her kids to experience it all.

How you can use this

I've saved what is perhaps the most important type of respect for here: respect for yourself. Traveling creates numerous challenges in terms of proper sleep, diet, exercise, caring for family, time to relax, and much more. Yet, so do our everyday lives no matter where we live. When is the last time you did something just for you? When is the last time you said "no" to an unreasonable request so you could spend more time doing what is important to you? Do you feel as though you treat your needs with the same respect as you treat the needs of your spouse, your children, and your boss? If you feel as though taking care of yourself adds just one more task to your already busy schedule, then ease into this concept gently. Each day, for just fifteen minutes, do something that is just about you. Sit quietly. Listen to your favorite music. Read a book. Do something that is purely to treat yourself with respect and love.

At the end of the day, we can train ourselves to be courteous to anyone. It doesn't take self-respect to offer courtesy. It does, however, take self-respect to find value in the way others do things differently than we do them. It takes self-respect to listen to the concerns of friends and to not judge them through our own cultural lens. It takes self-respect to fight back against people who would harm us for being different, and to recognize the sanity and sanctity of another culture's approach to life. Self-respect is the key to finding the hidden beauties in life. Not the beauties we have seen, but the ones that really have been hidden from us. In order to find those new beautiful moments, we must find the core that we appreciate most within ourselves and explore it, revel in it, and above all never forget it.

FOUR

Give Until Your Dreams Come True

We make a living by what we get,
but we make a life by what we give.

—Winston Churchill

egarding the chapter title, my children have told me that the famous Aerosmith song really says, "*Dream* Until Your Dreams Come True," but I hope you will forgive me for taking a bit of creative license in naming this chapter. For me, giving is a dream, but I'll be quick to confess not a purely unselfish one.

Giving of our time, money, and other resources runs deeply in both mine and Steve's families. As a child, I helped my grandmother prepare Bundles for Britain during World War II, and this and many other endeavors helped lay the groundwork for our immediate family's powerful vol-

Stevie, Casey Key, FL 2007.

unteer work as we journeyed to different spots around the globe. Volunteering to raise money, host parties, help whoever needed helping, though, also gave me a valuable way to make new friends in each new spot and to re-anchor our family. It plugged me in with like-minded expats, as well as the lifelong residents of each new country we explored.

Volunteering also gave me an alternative to helping beggars and the other less-aggressive needy in cultures where begging is a part of the social structure. India leaps to mind; on the one hand, my cultural background made me reluctant to "encourage" the begging. On the other hand, it was very difficult to walk past children needing life's basics. Or children whose parents threatened to beat them if they came back empty-handed from their quest. One little girl in particular always got a rupee or two from me for that very reason.

So when I was given the opportunity to contribute in what I felt to be a meaningful way, I leapt upon it. My Indian friend Goolie was of a Parsi family. Parsis are, in many cases, the corporate leaders of India. Parsis are prone to seeing a need and then cajoling their friends and fellow professionals into helping to find a place to solidify their response to the identified need.

In Bombay, however, there is no unused space. None. Consequently, when Goolie was anxious to start a school for the pathway children (their words for homeless) who lived along the Airport Road, she scouted out the neighborhood with her driver and saw an opportunity to use a garden in the median of the busy highway road to start her school. It had the benefit of a police box—a tiny neighborhood police station.

The narrow, grassy garden with lush borders of bougainvillea and shade trees was fenced in and had a water supply. The only drawback was the terrible fumes generated by the smoke-belching trucks and tuk-tuks (taxis). The small cache of supplies consisting of slates and chalk, a few books, and grass mats was kept in a trunk chained to a tree. Elements of personal hygiene were regular components of the school day, and every child had two changes of clothes, one drying at school and one to wear home. Goolie hired the nearby restaurant that supplied the police their tiffin lunch boxes stacked with bowls of food to do the same for the teachers and children.

The system of delivering lunch in tiffins is complex but completely satisfying, and I believe singularly specific to India. No man carries his lunch. The tiffin is collected after he leaves for work, put on the train along with thousands of others and delivered by illiterate laborers on bicycles to the man's office. The laborers "read" the color codes. I have never once heard of the wrong tiffin appearing.

We hired the nearby fruit vendor to supply everyone in the park with a banana every day. We found a teacher and a pediatrician friend of Goolie's to come once a month to check the children and advise the mothers on birth control. I always brought Henry, my extraordinary driver whom I hired because of his good nature, judgment and enthusiasm for knowledge and everything I was interested in. He played soccer with the children. They would have preferred cricket, but we had no way of keeping the ball within bounds as the traffic whizzed by. (Remember, we were between two very major and busy roads.)

I taught English and singing to the children once a week. The outdoor classroom was rearranged for every activity by moving the long grass mats in different conformations: in rows going back for class work and in a square for lunch and singing. The children had beautiful manners and could set an example for our spoiled Western children. They silently washed hands before lunch and took their places quietly with hands folded until the volunteers and teacher had scooped out lunches for all. We said grace, and the children ate slowly, enjoying their food until it was gone. No one ever threw food or played with it. There was a reverence in this partaking not seen in everyday life in the United States.

Actually, that is not completely true. If not actual reverence, the folks at St. Luke's in Stamford, Connecticut, seemed highly appreciative of all the good things that came their way; there was no taking anything for granted there, certainly. We ran St. Luke's after-school program, food bank, summer camp, and clothing exchange, which were enthusiastically patronized by many who lived on the south side of Stamford. Working to support that poor population was a refreshing respite from the white-gloved atmosphere in nearby Greenwich.

Yes. Even in our own country, volunteer work was a godsend because the children and I together had the opportunity to be a part of the reality of improvement and advancement in a community near our home. Perhaps our thought that returning to the United States would be easy was really what made returning so difficult. We were definitely changed by our experiences in the third world. What I do know is that my children and I felt like foreigners, a bit like a member of King Arthur's court in the dining room of a Connecticut Yankee when we first returned to the United States. But it was through the close interaction with our less-fortunate neighbors that we found a purpose and place in our community. I brought them to the museum, where I was art curator, for every exhibition and they were so reverential, asking questions that challenged the docents, who appreciated the real attention these kids gave the works on display. It was a tentative melding of our neighborhoods. The children found a home in the United States through the process of building relationships not only with the affluent children of Greenwich, but with the poor kids of South Stamford. Where both situations were new for them, they recognized the disparities between the two towns and found a way to fit in to both.

Beau's Perspective

Mom could have taken Greenwich by storm and forced us to fit in; she had the social skills to do so. Instead, though, when she saw us floundering, she moved in a new direction and helped us find friends we could relate to. And she cemented yet again the importance of helping others in the process, counterbalancing some of the influence of the Greenwich community. The family volunteer work eventually led to the basement becoming an apartment for a family of refugees, a mother and her two young daughters from El Salvador. Mom hired some men to build it out, and we furnished it out of our own house and partly through the swap at the church. It was brightly painted, as it had only a few windows, and Mom wanted the girls to be happy there.

The family settled in and my parents didn't charge rent for the first couple of years. The two girls quickly learned English and integrated nicely as scholars into Greenwich public schools. The mother, Blanca, found work and a boy-friend, and began her American life. Mom worked with the church to place refugees all throughout Greenwich. I helped her with this, taking weekends to load furniture, paint, collect donations, and talk with the children of the inbound families. Mom worked on at least four placements, maybe more. I was with her for all of them. It was a big lesson for me, I realize now, and kept me humble, grateful, and in close proximity to the church. Pretty smart lady, my mom.

How you can use this

So many times we'll beat our heads against the wall to reach our objective. Take a moment to step back and reflect what your true objective is. In my case, I was less concerned about adapting to Greenwich than I was in having my children happy and well adjusted. I looked for and found a different, more effective path to reach that goal. What goals are elusive to you? Are you certain you've identified them properly? What other ways can you reach them?

My volunteer work in Greenwich also allowed me to flex my art history and museum muscles, and I enjoyed using my formal training from Tokyo and London at the Bruce Museum. While at the museum, I curated the permanent collection, which was more accurately described as the attic for Greenwich because the major New York museums claimed all of the important works. With the registrar my first task was to deaccession damaged or inappropriate items from the collection and to hold an auction with several other Fairfield County institutions.

Twenty plus moose and ibex heads, trunks full of World War I gas masks, broken frames, and chimpanzee artwork sold for a grand total of about seventy thousand dollars over the three-day event. I'll never forget the country auctioneer who taught us all a thing or two by start-ing the first day by auctioning off a one-dollar coin for ten dollars! ("Get 'em in the mood," he said.)

After the auction my job was mounting exhibitions, six a year. Some were easily done: picking up carousel animals in our rental truck with our director in his blue coveralls stitched with "Jack" in gold on the pocket. The installation team was learning with every exhibition.

We did a Henry Moore lithograph show that I was able to augment by a collection of maquettes (small working versions of the larger sculpture) and a companion exhibition of Japanese tea bowls. The New York papers gave us great reviews and our clientele was soon augmented by visitors from New York City.

We mounted the first-in-the-world exhibition of robotics, which had the fire marshal very worried because attendance was so high. The same was true with the Energy in Sculpture exhibit with perhaps twenty large sculptures each moving by a different energy source.

I had a solid and active exhibitions committee, which worked hard to find and borrow antique toys in our community. We mounted three Christmas rooms behind glass, and I have to admit using a lot of our own furniture as stage sets for the eighteenth-, nineteenth- and early-twentieth-century collections of toys.

I was distraught collecting the items for the Benin masks exhibition when I realized we didn't have enough even for our small gallery. So that night at a drinks party I found some friends with Ashanti counter gold weights to lend and two of the largest collectors of African art in America willing to lend substantial pieces requiring us to completely rewrite our handout for the show. The Rockefeller wing personnel were all over that exhibition and tried every way to find out where we had borrowed these rare pieces. For the seventy hours a week I worked I was paid for fourteen, so it was mostly a volunteer job.

When we left Greenwich for Saudi Arabia, volunteer work took yet another turn, this time in the form of writing a travel book on Dir'aiyah, the ancient citadel of the Al Saud when they were formalizing plans for expansion and saw the Wahhabi sect of Sunni Islam as an asset to their goals. The Wahhabi, who actually were the first occupants of our palace in Dir'aiyah in the eighteenth century, were located across the wadi, the dry river bed, from the Al Saud Citadel. By the twentieth century the citadel was in disrepair, eroding from occasional rains and blowing winds across the desert.

On Fridays (read Sundays) Korean road workers would come for picnicking at the citadel. They stood looking for answers at what they were seeing to the point that I thought I should write a book about the ruins. I asked Didi Cutler, a friend and wonderful photographer with a new Hasselblad camera, to take the photographs for the book. Every publisher we approached wanted to publish it for either one thousand UK pounds or American dollars. None would let me make artistic decisions, which was the part I couldn't agree with.

Steve finally said he would publish it, even though I warned that publishers were all in agreement that it would never sell five-thousand copies. He said, "So we'll print ten thousand!" We sold out in thirteen months and grossed forty-five thousand dollars wholesaling it to stores and the shop at the ruins. Subsequently I gave the rights to publish my book and sell it for their own projects to the Saudi Princess' Charity jointly with the American Women's Club. I stipulated that the same paper and layout be used to which they agreed. However, when I finally saw their version on poor paper with advertising throughout, I was sorry I had given permission to use my name.

How you can use this

No matter where you live, people need your help. The United States seems filled today with lonely singles looking for mates, with retiring and restless baby boomers, and with a general malaise that stems at least in part from a lack of a sense of community. Volunteering gets you off your sofa, takes you away from your computer, helps you meet people, and helps other people, too. Win, win, win. You can't do any better than that.

Let Us Entertain You

Throughout our travels, but perhaps in Saudi Arabia in particular, the ability to nurture and support our family, friends, and colleagues deserves to be set apart from the other opportunities I had to enjoy their companionship. Entertaining for me was always a way to connect with family and friends, as well as to charm Steve's colleagues. This desire to charm once led me to buy an eighty-dollar pot roast in Tokyo, news of which quickly buzzed through the expat community where hushed whispers of the feat greeted me upon my arrival at an art event the following day.

Pricey pot roast aside, Saudi Arabia stands out in my mind even more since we had an entire desert to frolic in with our events. And frolic we did, albeit under the watchful eye of the Saudis who would perch on a hilltop and observe us with ominous energy pouring forth from them.

Beau's Perspective

In what may be the most repressively anti-Western culture I have experienced, Mom and her friends put together a scavenger hunt that took eight expat families across the city and the desert in search of the most bizarre set of objects. It culminated in a huge party out in an escarpment outside of Riyadh. The adults drank wine, the kids snuck beer and embassy-guaranteed Western sodas. We all wore hats decorated in strange ways, laughed with one another, and celebrated the good company that we were able to create. I was given a driving lesson in a Land Rover. I was thirteen years old.

A favorite event was a scavenger hunt to the desert once offered by two families and named the "Wilbercockie." We hid clues along the route to directions cryptically rhyming for the next checkpoint. The prize was arriving at the party location deep in the desert. Once there, women drove blindfolded on the desert, and we played other games and had lunch. Each family group was assigned a famous group to portray in a homemade skit. Good friends came dressed as the Sex Pistols in Gothic splendor, and they won first prize. But on the way home they were stopped by the Saudi police, having to explain exactly why they looked as they did.

At home in Dir'aiyah, Steve often brought visiting international bankers to lunch with our family in our separate, mud-house kitchen with two connecting dining rooms of enormous proportions. We usually only set one table at lunch—for up to ten people. Once, our cook, Hassan, had cooked what was believed to be the best beef stew we had ever had. However, against Hassan's advice I told them we were eating camel! The children were disgusted, Steve turned green, and from that day forward no matter what was delivered to the table, Ashley would slide her eyes up to Hassan and ask, "Is this camel, Hassan?" So we went through that rite of passage daily much to the amusement of the guests.

Often Iman, our Bangladeshi houseboy, would step beyond his usual decorum by running into the dining room yelling, "The goats are in the rose garden!" At which we would leap to action with our dinner napkins flapping and calling the guests to action to drive the herd out of the rose garden and down the long driveway to the road. It was a memorable day out for the visitors. The emir told me I should have one of the goats in payment for all of the trespassing the herd did. So we organized a rope and one day caught a goat that I couldn't hold—they are enormously strong—and we never had goats in the garden again.

How you can use this

I know many people who are terrified at the thought of entertaining. My attitude is that it's not about you, but rather your guests. As a guest, though, you should be thinking the opposite: it's about entertaining your host's other guests, not being entertained by them. I always enjoyed being able to broaden my guests' experiences by introducing them to each other and seeing new friendships blossom. Creating a sense of surprise is important, so even in a house party, moving from one venue within the house to another is important. Keep things stirred up a bit. Finally, working with themes helps. I've hosted a Tennis Ball, where the guests played tennis then donned evening clothes to dance the night away during a formal ball; a Gone with the Wind Ball; and a Non-Ball Ball that created quite a stir by the absence of an actual ball. Your imagination is the only limit, so enjoy!

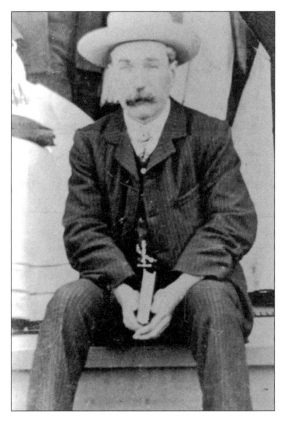

Stevie's grandfather, James Mein, 1900.

FIVE

Take a Walk
on the Wild Side

Art flourishes where there is a sense of adventure.

—Alfred North Whitehead

A sense of adventure is in my blood—quite literally handed down from my grandparents to me. My lineage and my own travel-lust made me particularly adaptable to the overseas lifestyle required by Steve's job, and I tried to teach our children to see the playful adventure involved in our moves and our travels, even during challenging situations. I hope I have handed down that sense of adventure and travel to my own children. By living in various places around the world, and especially for doing so because of Steve's Merrill Lynch job, I realized that I've had the opportunity to fulfill the goals of my grandparents. My grandmother loved to travel, and my earliest memories of a newspaper was sitting on my grandfather's lap as he read the *Wall Street Journal* to me and me to him for his amusement.

To describe it as a mindset greatly understates the overall picture of embracing adventure. And embracing the unknown is a vital part of truly enjoying—instead of merely tolerating—the adventures you find yourself in. Learning how to create adventure out of the mundane rituals of being in a new location, or even in everyday life, is HUGE. Beyond just tolerating what is going on around you, proactively seeking to make both everyday and unique situations more fun and more rewarding enables you to grab life and all it has to offer with gusto.

Daily life in other countries, though, frequently provides unintentional adventure. In India, just a walk down the street meant literally walking down the street because the sidewalks were jammed with hopeful entrepreneurs: barbers, the man with his typewriter, the coconut salesman, the cobbler, a makeshift Ferris wheel with four seats (clearly they don't have the same aversion to the number four as the Japanese do).

In the morning the street dwellers got up and did their ablutions on the pavement, brushing their teeth and bathing, having folded their blanket on their pallet and stowed it in a tree. Many slept on the streets in Bombay, but they didn't freeze. Almost all cultures can provide for the most basic needs of their people. One man sold tea and rolls along the pavement each morning. There was always a water spigot, and almost any food can be bought from temporary stalls. Homeless did not mean jobless.

Traffic flows at a slow pace in Bombay. Drivers watch out for what is falling off the vehicle ahead: a sari-clad woman falling off the back of the family motor scooter or an avalanche of melons, for instance. Potholes are of legendary proportion, so chaos is assured. And a sacred cow was always in the fast lane, moving when she wanted or when an exasperated driver nudged her with his fender.

Daily life in other countries meant hobnobbing with royalty and a different sort of adventure. For example, we had a front row view of Princess Di and Charles' wedding procession. Watching the traffic jam procession of perspiring diplomats, comedians, and others passing their hats for spare change readily supplied by the common man along the way, and the poor policemen dotting the route passing out from heat added to the carnival atmosphere.

Ashley's Perspective

Meeting the Queen

London was a magical time, throughout the many years—in and out—that we were there.

Occasionally, there was someone from the Royal Family involved in what we were doing.

I remember the day that Princess Di was married. We were invited to the bank of close friends to view the parade out from the building's second-floor balconies as they passed by on the street below. The density of people was impressive. We waved and cheered as the princess passed on her way to St. Paul's Cathedral.

There were more royal sightings when we went to Wimbledon. Merrill Lynch hosted a corporate tent, and we grazed on strawberries and cream, and sips of champagne between matches. Wimbledon smells like berries and freshly mowed grass. We saw John McEnroe play, and we people-watched the Royal Box with all the family coming and going.

Mom and I attended the Royal College of Music's sponsored evening at St. James's Palace where we had a spectacular black-tie evening with Paul McCartney and friends in the presence of HRH The Prince of Wales. *The Leaf,* McCartney's first solo work for classical piano, was memorable, along with Elvis Costello, and the Brodsky Quartet. I wore my black dress that had black and white ruffles all over it—something that you only feel comfortable wearing if your mommy reassures you that "that is *it!* Perfect"—and we felt like princesses at the palace. The very handsome young man sitting to my left kept telling me how beautiful my dress was. But then we looked at his date in a see-through chiffon blouse and realized he was mortified by this obviously uncomfortable young woman.

On a separate occasion, Mom had an invitation to St. James's Palace for the Pilgrim's Reception. Mom and I wore our prettiest dresses and chapeaus and off we went to the palace to have a reception with the Queen. When we arrived at the palace we were ushered in with several hundred other people into the Queen Anne Room. Tapestries hung on the walls, antique furniture, portraits—ornate details throughout. It felt like we should have been expecting a palace tour guide to appear and explain all the glory of the room.

Instead, there was an announcement that the Queen was here. Hush filled the room. It was hard to see her perfectly through the sea of hats, movements, bows and curtsies, but I saw her and she was glorious in her powdery suit; I knew that I was living a most special, singular evening with my mom and the Queen.

Onnie, Stevie, and Ashley, near Florence, Italy, 1979.

Living abroad gave us a chance to see America's own celebrities more readily, too. When Van was eight in London, he was having a very difficult time seeing why it was good to be an American. Ronald Reagan helped fix that.

Ronald and Nancy Reagan came to town, and Steve and I were giving the party to introduce him to American Republicans at a big hotel. Steve called from Brussels that he had missed the plane, so I asked Van to get on his blazer and help me out.

We went to the back room where we expected twenty to thirty high rollers because the Reagans were to spend an hour there. Then Ronald was to speak to a large crowd of perhaps five hundred in the ballroom. Ronnie made the rounds at the party and then asked me if there was anything in particular he could do with the last twenty minutes. I told him about Van and that he was so down in the dumps about being an American and why.

Ronnie literally rubbed his hands together and went to sit with him, talked for several minutes, and then asked Van to have his picture made with him and Nancy. Van remembers this kindly man telling him that he, Van, was an American hero standing up for his country, that it was difficult for him to be living far from home, but that we have a wonderful country that looks after the rest of the world, and sometimes they don't like it.

Ronnie took the pin from his own lapel with crossed flags of Great Britain and the United States and pinned it on Van's blazer. Such a gesture was perhaps the most important thing he accomplished that night, as a dozen years later Van went on to volunteer for four years in the U.S. Army and to become a highly successful diplomat and government official, always a Republican and a proud American from that day.

And then there was seeing Anthony Blunt's last lecture at Christie's before he was de-knighted. He gave a lovely lecture about the Queen's art collection, got into a cab, and was never seen again.

A Friend's Perspective

Julia Moore, an Englishwoman and animal lover

Perhaps the maddest of Stevie's schemes, but the one that reduced us both to quivering jellies of hysterical laughter, was her plan to write a book of walks and research it during monsoon season in India. Nobody had ever attempted such a crazy thing because all self-respecting Bombay-wallas prefer a local hero in a 4x4 to take them from A to B. It was Henry—Steve and Stevie's local hero, and what a sweet man he was, who would drop us at our start point and then be given instructions for the pick up several miles away! We then set off carrying our umbrellas and notepads to do our research . . .

We branched left down Bank Street, all the while attracting interest from the locals as we wrote down points on our notepads. The Turner Morrison Building on the next corner impressed us enormously. We had observed the original features and excellent condition of the interior and had to know more about Mr. Turner or Mr. Morrison. We strode in and were directed to the first-floor office of Turner & Morrison itself where we found ourselves in a Parsi haven. A charming elderly lady came to our assistance and after leaving our umbrellas in the excellent charge of Jacob we were ushered into the general manager's office. He delved into his archives and produced a file about the building's origins and gladly answered our searching questions!

Our research took us down every smelly alley in south Bombay. We engaged numerous bewildered locals, we were chased by stray dogs, and one day we sat outside a rat hospital to rest our weary legs! Above all, we had a huge laugh. But just as the book was beginning to take shape a local historian got wind of our plan and within a few weeks had written, with his staff of a dozen writers, his own book of walks. He, of course, missed every smelly alley. Missing were the cow barns and the nearby tiny Buddha temple: not that the temple was small, but the Buddha was minuscule requiring worshippers to bring binoculars. That's India for you!

Stevie walks as if there is a bouncy carpet beneath her feet. She is the perkiest girl I know and I'd go anywhere with her.

Another Prespective from Julia Moore

Stevie is such a one for coming up with brilliant ideas. She enlisted me as her aide and what a laugh we had. One of these ideas was creating a game called Mumbopoly! It was Bombay's answer to Monopoly, complete with squatters' hutments (the owner had to pay the squatter to leave) and hilarious forfeit cards. Every copy sold and serious money was raised for local charities. Even the British Museum insisted on a copy for their games archives—incredible girl, that Stevie! Her passion and vitality made this project a fascinating journey, and she was a joy to work with.

Ashley's Perspective

It's not always the big, dramatic things that create adventure and a sense of mystery. My mom was always really good at creating the little surprises that made life fun. For example, when we lived in London, she'd walk me home from Lady Eden's School, holding my hand as I skipped along. Sometimes we'd stop and feed the ducks at Holland or Hyde Park. Other times we'd go to Action Park—an obscenely dangerous playground of rope swings, balance-beam plank walks high in the trees, and netting to climb. Then we might, if it was a particularly lucky day, stop off for an ice-cream cone with a rabbit ear (chocolate bar).

One day, Mom surprised me by taking me to the Ritz Carlton for tea. It was the most beautiful dining room in Europe, with a golden ceiling with extraordinary detail. There were angels and ornate china, scrumptious scones, and the whole experience felt like a storybook fantasy.

Random tests of fortitude while exploring

Bamako, the capital of Mali, is a very organized African capital, with good roads and mended potholes that is on the banks of the Niger River. The national museum is incredibly modern with good exhibitions of traditional artifacts. We traveled north by small SUV, with driver and guide, to many villages and towns that were never very far from the Niger River, and we arrived in Timbuktu at Christmastime.

Van's Perspective

We spent Christmas in Morocco one year, where our family traveled from the better-established northern coasts into the less-developed south, which joins with the Sahara desert. Our plans included staying in a five-star hotel on the edge of the desert, to enable us to see the sun rise in the early morning.

The five-star hotel was a massive complex with dirty sheets and other challenges. We happily slept in our own clothes. At three thirty in the morning we rose, and joined our driver in his car. Prior to leaving, however, he took five minutes to say prayers for safety in this treacherous desert with no set road. We drove in near total blackness, venturing further into the desert. At some point, we stopped driving and walked to an open-air lodge. The sky was starting to lighten, and in the predawn we could make out the dimensions of this "zero star" waypoint. We were all wearing all of our clothes from our suitcase as it was well below freezing with howling winds.

We walked further toward towering dunes and the sun started to rise. All of us, pulled by the beauty, moved further toward the sun, leg muscles straining as we climbed one dune after the next. Oranges and reds blazed in the sky. No one complained about the great cold, but Mom offered some of her layers to her children, including me. I got a sleeveless fur jacket, suitable for a very fashionable woman!

Once beyond settlements in Mali, the roads were virtually deserted. Large escarpments hung in the distance. Seas of long grass bent in the wind. We stayed in a wonderful mud-brick-and-thatched-hut hotel in Djenné overnight. Around the corner from the hotel is a

World Heritage site, the largest mud-brick edifice in the world. It was massive and cleverly designed so that repairs could be done by all the villagers at once, with details designed to be actual stepping places to the highest points of the structure. The decoration includes crennolation—one peak on each roof for each child, and on the ground in front there is one toadstool shape for each wife, according to local tradition.

We bought many postcards to send as Christmas cards and wrote: "Merry Christmas from Timbuktu." (We had to get the postcards from wherever we could, whether or not it was technically Timbuktu proper). When we went to the post office to buy stamps for the postcards, the aging postal worker shook his head and suggested there was wasted space on every card and would I like to take them back to rectify this mistake? Embarrassed, I said no, it was a little memento for each friend. Eyes widening, he looked me in the eye and lectured me on the price.

Outside, it was market day. We returned to the hotel and stood on the roof of one of the huts and watched the laden donkey carts rush across the desert from every direction to be the first to reach a shaded spot in the market square.

We looked around the stalls, which sold fruits, bread, meals, huge gold earrings, and artistic items. I chose five little handmade low-fired clay animals. Our guide sniffed at my choice. "We made those in elementary school," he scoffed.

I wasn't scoring any points in Djenné! Such a gentle clash of cultures over such small incidents.

An hour later we drove into Dogonland (Bandigara district). We drove a very good road to Sanga, but it turned into half a road halfway there, making passing oncoming vehicles very difficult, as no one wanted to give up their purchase on the road. In Dogonland, Ahmadu, our guide, introduced us to a medicine man, a goldsmith and a blacksmith.

We hiked a long way as pied pipers with a gathering collection of stray children who were selling us their lunch and even their school papers. They were good natured and chatty, but disappointed that their times tables weren't bringing in any cash. (So much for education!)

The village of Amani had a wonderful, shaded fetid crocodile pond. We stayed around in the cool watching the eighty crocs and a group of old men fishing for lunch, while Ahmadu explained how the villagers all wear gold amulets to protect them from the bite of the crocs.

Then the inevitable happened, and we had a chance to test the theory. One fisherman snagged a large fish that took the pole with him. This indeed was a predicament that instigated a loud meeting of the gesturing elders who each had an idea, all simultaneously expressed. He must retrieve his pole, a prized possession. Ahmadu said the crocs protect the old men, so why was this toothless old man worried? (Why indeed!) The old man undressed, plunged in, and got his pole back, and the catfish, and scampered out. The crocs never blinked an eye. He was a hero for a day.

The Sanga people had a definitive way of making decisions. The village chief had a fox as his spiritual guide, and he communicated his questions on one of three sorts of hopscotch boards drawn in the clay. A villager might want to know if he should marry a certain girl, if she should leave home to work in the big city, or any other worrisome problem. They went to the chief, who then made a series of little marks and mounds in the clay, added stones and twigs in specific spots, and waited overnight for the fox to come to rearrange these items. In the morning the chief read the fox's decision. Villagers always followed this advice as it made perfect sense to them.

We were on our way to Timbuktu, a place I had always wanted to visit ever since our Christmas in Morocco in the 1980s when we drove to the end of a road where it finished in the desert. At the end of the road was a sign: "52 days by camel to Timbuktu." Such a welcoming challenge! So there we were twenty years later making that trip, fulfilling a dream.

Steve's Perspective

The Law of Diminishing Expectations

The night journey across the border was an excellent example of the Law of Diminishing Expectations. When we finally arrived at our hotel, sometime after two in the morning, we learned that the hotel had no electricity or running water. Absolutely exhausted we tried to follow the directions of the concierge who was pointing in the direction of the corner of the large room that served as all-purpose entry, reception, café restaurant, and based upon the dozen or so curled up upon the benches and snoring loudly, a dormitory for the homeless. The unoccupied bench in the corner indicated had a three inch foam pad over it. Clearly it was the VIP bench.

Stevie looked at it and said "Oh, that's nice. It looks quite comfortable." The clerk showed us past the corner through the sliding glass doors and on to a series of cabanas, one of which was ours. After a quick check for mosquito netting (passable) and snakes (none) we collapsed in our clothes on filthy sheets.

It wasn't too bad, but it was a palace in relation to the corner bench in the homeless shelter. That is the law of Diminished Expectations. If you want to see something in a different light, do without it for a while.

We were required to use a ferry to cross the Niger River, and found ourselves in a two-mile-long queue. The president would be arriving in Timbuktu in a few days to view the arts presentation there, creating havoc on the roads.

We stopped overnight, staying in the same room that the president of would be sleeping in. Breakfast was the usual Arabic bread and Nescafé, the crystals served in a narrow sealed package. I asked Ahmadu, our guide, how they managed to always get the sand inside the bread. We walked around the town, which had venerated three foreigners who came across the Sahara to discover Timbuktu by naming a museum after each of them. Aside from a few mosques of slim interest and a garish bazaar, there was little to visit, and we focused on the people. We suddenly realized we kept seeing the same people over and over, like a movie with a limited number of extras.

We decided I should make an entrance into Timbuktu by camel and so we went to the camel stand to arrange it. The Tuareg men in blue-and-white shirts over their jeans and heads wrapped in turbans and face scarves ran the camels. The man who led me had been to Timbuktu with a group of elders who were passing the tradition on to their grandsons. They moved from well to well through the desert only by night because the stars guided them. I asked him how long it took them. Without hesitation he said fifty-two days!

We went to a desert encampment where the women sat in the sand behind the tents. They, of course, had jewelry for sale. One counseled me, "You should buy something to help the village." I have seen too much to be fooled by this obvious mind game. I said I would buy something because I liked it, but to help the village I would give money to "Save the Children" where Ahmadu's mother worked a large area on a motor scooter. I did buy some interesting tassels, which made everyone happy.

We left our hotel early because we had been given the room where the president (called ATT by his people) was to stay that night for the opening of the crafts festival.

We were now on our way to Niger. At one ferry crossing point at the village of Gao, we discovered that the ferry driver had closed shop early. We went around town looking for him, eventually discovering him at home. It took twenty-five minutes to negotiate with him to return to work so that we could cross the river. We sat in the Jeep while the guide spoke with the ferryman. At each stage of the negotiation, the guide would return to our Jeep to explain what was happening. Effectively, this was a negotiation over the amount to bribe him to return to work. The sum we arrived at was less than ten dollars.

Crossing into Niger the next night was difficult. Our driver and guide could not find the crossing point. Along the way, we stopped a shepherd—an old man with white whiskers in a white robe—to ask for directions. After some conversation, he entered the car and directed us near the crossing in the extreme dark. He could locate the crossing

Stevie on Hats

Few things announce your confidence like wearing a good hat properly.

The place to find a hat is in a horse-racing town, such as Saratoga. The smart hat-shop owner always asks if you are buying a hat for the "Winner's Circle." I always answer "No, it's for my daughter's wedding," or some such thing, and she is quick to enthuse, "Why, then it *is* for the winner's circle." Don't perch your hat on your head: Fit it to your head, and drop back in first. This prevents hat head and is the method the Queen of England uses (have you ever seen the Queen with hat head?).

Balance your hat properly or wearing it will tire you.

It is best to find a bespoke hat, one that is "made for you," a one-of-a-kind hat.

Vary how you wear your hats and what types of hats you wear. You can wear a hat and jeans, as a dear friend of mine does. Wear some that are taller, some that are wider, etc. Wear interesting colors, and understand that you don't have to match. You can blend. Most importantly, pay three hundred dollars minimum for a hat or you'll meet yourself coming and going.

point by reading the stars. (He stuck his head out of the car window, and would occasionally offer directions in a quiet voice.)

After arriving at the crossing point, the shepherd said good-bye and walked back to his flock, finding his way by the stars. He asked for no compensation for the trouble, seemingly happy to help lost tourists.

Once across the Mali border, armed men in uniform surrounded our car. We were told to get out of the car while the military examined our luggage. After two hours, we were permitted to cross the border into Niger. (The Malian government was having trouble with Tuareg rebels, and this may have been a tense time.) In the light we returned to the crossing to verify what our memories told us: the border consisted of a loose dirt road with no established track and a wooden branch lifted and lowered to open and close the road.

Confidence creates adventure

Or does adventure create confidence? A relationship definitely exists. Being comfortable with who you are, no matter where you are, was something I worked hard to teach my children. And in turn, our family philosophy of charging ahead created new adventures and new ways to test that confidence and instill yet more.

To us, confidence means being willing to step into new, unknown situations, sometimes with little or no information, and knowing everything will turn out okay. The more you seek adventures to exercise your confidence muscles, the more confident you become, and the more you will in turn seek out those adventures.

Van's Perspective

Mom is always up for adventure, and this broadened my own view of the world considerably. My mom and I went to Yemen in 1989 during Christmas break. We arrived in Sana'a during one of the country's periods of civil war. As we traveled throughout the northern half of the country, we were stopped at military checkpoints about every twenty miles, which definitely added an element of adventure to the trip.

Our driver, Ali, was a gregarious know-it-all, which Mom tolerated for the most of the trip. On one occasion, Ali repeatedly asked me to try typical Yemeni breakfast, which I finally did. Mom said in no uncertain terms this was a bad idea intestinally since I did not have the established antibodies to tolerate local cuisine!

We brought jars of peanut better in case we couldn't eat the food. I remember expeditions in several towns, hunting for Yemeni flat bread to eat with the peanut butter.

Mom was very brave. The further north we traveled, the more we saw machine guns (Russian AK-47s) in the hands of the public. At one very well-known archaeological site where we stopped, a crowd of children armed to the teeth joined us. I smiled and waved to these "nice" gun-toting children, who actually were very pleasant. At gas stations where we stopped, old men smoking cigarettes would fill up our car, for five cents a gallon.

The locals consume a narcotic called khat or ghat. We saw evidence of ghat everywhere we went on the roadside. Ali bought a branch every day, which he would chew well into the afternoon. As Ali was our driver, this habit bothered Mom, but she did not mention her concern because it was a locally established custom, even though it could be dangerous.

Yemen is world renowned for its ancient skyscrapers, ten-story buildings made of stone and brick, which is not evidenced in other parts of the ancient world.

Zimbabwe also provided adventure for us when my family arranged a week's canoe paddle down the Zambezi River. We rowed twenty-five kilometers a day, much of it against the wind. We couldn't take baths because the river was shallow, concentrating the crocodiles in the shallows and the hippos in the deeper pools so they could submerge. After one long day's row to Mana Pools, our first stop, it was clear to my mother that the trip was not appropriate for my grandmother. At night, we zipped up our tents to keep the roving hyenas from eating our faces.

It is important to note how dangerous hippos are on African rivers. They are intensely protective of their children, as well as being very territorial. More deaths are attributed to hippos every year than to other dangerous animals in

Africa. We called this canoe trip the "hippo slalom," given the requirement to dodge families of hippos on one bank or another (or in the deeper pools).

Though Beau doesn't remember it, my dad remembers that Beau had his first offer of marriage at the age of fourteen. We were fishing on the Zambian shore when the headman of the village came to see what was going on. He coveted Beau's rod and actually offered to trade his eldest daughter for it!

It takes a lot of confidence to bring your kids on adventures like this, and Mom was definitely up for the task.

On our Zambezi trip we stayed at the Mana Pools campsite near the communications/ranger station, having waved the men off down the river. We had been given some food for lunch, which came before noon. Men working nearby were killing snakes and brought them to show us. We wrote in our diaries and looked at the birds until Rukomechi camp had its airtime at 3:00 P.M. We asked if we could come back for a few days and regroup. They sent a vehicle for us and in two hours we were on our way back to beloved Rukomechi, with its cabins in a circle, its bathtubs on the river, and the dining room in a lean-to, also on the river.

There was a huge bull elephant named Joseph back in camp after his long day in the forest. It was a coincidence that Rukomechi was built in Joseph's path, but they each made accommodation for the other. No one ever fed Joseph, and he harmed nothing at camp unless the tempting fruit bowl was left out by mistake, and then that was fair game.

One evening, Ashley left the campfire to find the cabin in the dark, arms outstretched like a sleepwalker, and walked into Joseph who stood very still, allowing her hands to explore what she thought was a tree. It was such a brilliant demonstration of coexistence of acceptance and trust. Joseph never moved a muscle until Ashley headed toward her cabin.

The camp was full of a group of paddlers who had come out of Mana Pools after a lioness had attacked a young woman sleeping only under net, which we were all counseled against. This has by now become a famous story. Their guide was telling ours what had happened during the hours of fighting off the lioness. The group was hoarse and frantic, but chose to stay for group counseling even though their attacked friend had been taken out by helicopter to the airstrip and returned to South Africa, where she had surgery.

We asked for an alternative plan, and we gladly accepted and hired a plane to take us to Greater Zimbabwe and other sights, collecting the rest of the family at the Mozambique border. There, Steve and the boys took off their shirts and used them as wind socks to help us land, and were full of excited stories all the way back to Harare.

The group dispersed then, with Van going to his job at Camp Xax-aba, Onnie going home, Ashley to hockey camp, and Steve and I to Riyadh. I decided to get a last look at Cairo, though, because we were leaving Riyadh in six months. Beau headed to the British Virgin Islands for three weeks of scuba and sailing instruction.

The adventure is just the beginning

We went to Persia in the autumn of 2007, traveling with wonderful friends we made in Bombay and another Scottish couple who were cheerful and educated companions. We met at Heathrow, and it was an uneventful trip until we landed in Iran, and Steve and I were glee-fully singled out as American citizens. So at 1:00 A.M. the rest of our band of nomads waited patiently at the top of the stairs at the exit watching us get fingerprinted and extra-documented. After, we were allowed to use a very glamorous bathroom in which we washed our hands.

The hotels were beautiful spots obviously used for conventions and the few tourists, mostly Europeans, who came to appreciate Iran's ancient customs, buildings, and tile work so handily intertwined with poetry in a form of sophistication not known elsewhere.

Steve, for example, found a beautiful tile painting applied to the side of a building. He was curious because the birds in the tile painting held butterflies in their beaks—an unnatural gesture. Mohammed, our guide, asked for a minute to think about it. I should tell you that one of the great sports in Persia is taking an ancient poem and interpreting it. Back he came with an enlightened look: the birds holding the bugs and butterflies in their beaks represented illicit love.

The miniature paintings for many centuries past depict gardens of enormous beauty. So we were all anxious to spend time in them. The miniatures didn't do justice to the cascading waterfalls some 25 ft wide and thirty in number lined with rose bushes. The water cooled the air so well that we quickly forgot it was a hot day in the middle of a desert. Another was a series of walkways lined with high, pruned bushes that always kept us in the shade. Even a narrow strip of land was cleverly decorated to amuse the eye on a long walk to the front door of a building.

The ancient bazaars looked dangerous as their domes seemed fragile and ominous. Women in their black coats and head scarves were much freer to shoplift with such expansive cover. Shopkeepers were busy tracking down a few culprits at one. We visited baths (hot, cold, and warm rooms) in the bazaar and tea houses. The central squares are geometrically designed so that the domes and portals of one mosque and those of others took on different configurations. They were so complex that the puzzle of their placement was only solved in the last century.

Young school girls were curious about us since we were dressed modestly but not in standard mufti. They asked about our clothes and when they learned that we were from the United States they were so excited. We learned to say that we were from Los Angeles because it seemed as if everyone in Persia had a relative there. The coincidence was too exciting for them. The girls all had a little look that Mohammed sometimes had to translate. Poor Mohammed wanted a bride and that such a studious and sweet person at age thirty was still not married was such a puzzle to us! We started telling the girls that Mohammed needed a wife and his parents were liberals who wouldn't help him. We, his customers, could vouch for him but where would he meet the right girl? We never got further than calling one girl's English teacher who didn't want to know.

Wilberding family portrait, 1988. Clockwise from top left: Steve, Van, Beau, Ashley, and Stevie.

Van's Perspective

I had asked my parents not to go on their trip to Iran, which they were calling "Persia." I had explained several reasons why, including the fact that the Iranian government was probably involved in kidnapping Western nationals. My mother was annoyed with me (I suspect for my being small-minded). At one point, she said to my father, "Steve, Van says I can't go to Persia." I had the good sense not to raise the topic again.

Upon their return from Iran, it was interesting to watch how fulfilled my parents were from their visit. My mother described the Iranian people as "decent," "cultured," "welcoming" and "open." (She said some slightly unflattering things about George Bush, Jr., too.) My parents were both aware of the corrupt and authoritarian quality of the Iranian government, but saw this as distinct from the people, whom they clearly admired.

While I did not travel with them, I think this story is particularly revealing about the general value of travel. It makes us skeptical about dogma and common paradigms of our government, media, and people. It forces us to trust our own senses and instincts much more. Those who have traveled and seen with their own eyes seem to more clearly recognize the agendas of opinion-makers with respect to the rest of the world.

A Friend's Perspective

Cheryl Kyle

One day in 1996 my late husband and I sent an e-mail to Stevie inquiring about places she'd recommend for us to see in India. Without a second thought Stevie said to come to Mumbai and she and Steve would plan our trip when we arrived. We took her at her word and not long after, with tour book in hand, Pete and I left our home in Tegucigalpa, Honduras, picked up our daughter Camille and her husband, Matthew, at their home in Singapore, and headed to Mumbai.

We were met at the airport by their car and driver and whisked away to their mansion in the heart of Mumbai. Wow! We had arrived in a beautiful and artfully decorated home featuring amazing paintings, sculptures, and works in iron Stevie had collected in India. Naturally she knew the artists, their history, and they were now friends of hers. During our visit Stevie planned our trip, which included overnights in palaces, elephant rides, visits to historical temples—a trip we will always remember thanks to Stevie.

But what comes to mind when we think of Stevie and Steve is the five days we stayed in their home. A tour of Mumbai as only Stevie could give you from the central market, Elephant Island, red-light district, the central laundry area, art galleries, gemstone dealers, silk sari shops, and the Gateway to India Archway.

Central to our experience, however, was the warm hospitality given to four weary travelers. We were included at a dinner party at the U.S. Embassy, art receptions, a visit to the home of a maharaja, and our final evening in their home celebrating Thanksgiving and my birthday. A gift of a silver salad set made in India grace my table in Cape Cod. They will always remind me of Stevie and our visit to India and her visits to my cottage on the Cape. One thing we did with several guests was having have our fortunes told by reading our shadows,. It cost the equivalent of $45 and it was the specialty of the man down on the corner who sold rattan furniture on the side. One a sunny day he took you out on the pavement and measured the height, width, and length of your head and any manner of other possibilities. We'd troop back inside, usually giggling and ready for the scam. Sure enough, with a straight face he opened his well- thumbed books, consulted the numbers and began. "You were first a Japanese princess, but because of jealousy lost your life returning as an Afghani princess . . . etc." We had a jolly time categorizing our days which that followed by the kind of princess we felt like. A complete and utter scam—, too zany to make up. It only offended one Scottish woman, who wanted her money back!

I didn't want to be outdone, so when one day in 2003 or thereabouts, when Stevie e-mailed me at my home in Arusha, Tanzania, and said she was coming for a visit, I jumped at the opportunity to return the hospitality. Now I had the opportunity to show Stevie the sights I love so much and to introduce her to my friends. We had a mini safari to the game parks, toured a hybrid seed company with a Maasai friend, and visited my Maasai askari/guard's family in their boma. Stevie met and dined with many of my missionary friends in Arusha, we worshipped together, and spent time with the bishop and his wife. Her inquiring mind, laughter, and the joy she gets from traveling made our experience in Tanzania together a pleasure.

Nothing says confident like a yellow car

MARJORIE NORTH

I had missed my turn to do a few errands up the Tamiami Trail in Sarasota while driving in my boring old metallic gray BMW with every picture and dial known to man and a shark's fin on top. Suddenly on the left corner ahead slowly spun the most beautiful butter-yellow sports car.

I did a U-turn back to Chrysler and asked if I could test drive it.

"No, you can test drive the gray one," he said.

"I've driven my last gray car," I said.

"Then how about testing the white or black one?"

"Nope, not interested." I only wanted the yellow.

Brass and sass

That brassy **Stevie Wilberding** on her way to Calico Corners in her new, "dreary" gray, blank-name car, with a dorsel fin yet, missed the turn and spotted a yellow Crossfire on the turntable on the corner at Chrysler. She admits doing a u-ey, went in and told the salesman she wanted to test drive it, to which he responded, "You can test the gray one."

"Not on your life," Stevie said. "I have driven my last gray car."

Smart Chrysler folks took it off the turn table and Stevie took it after a quick drive. She got the car and a check for hers, at least enough to get a bling hat and sunglasses to go with the new car. There are some women you just don't ask to test-drive gray . . . you know what I mean?

I took the Crossfire for a spin, came back, and said I wanted it. "How much is it?"

When they told me, I said, "Well, my gray car is worth more!"

"Well, you get the car and the check!"

Of course the check was enough for a bling hat and sunglasses and a pair of red high heels . . . in satin. I've put a silk ribbon tassel on the key chain, and there are fresh flowers in the vase placed in the coffee cup holder. Such a happy solution.

Wilberforce

You know what you want. And then there's doing what you must to get it. For many, this is an insurmountable gap. For our family, it means knowing that you roll up your sleeves and work hard to get it. Ingenuity helps, so does sacrifice.

We taught our children the skills they need to succeed, and to accomplish what they want. This is all part of the family mindset that we call "Wilberforce." If something needs to be done, the family rallies and we make it happen.

One Christmas holiday when we were all together, Beau and Suki, his wife, decided they needed more space in their home. The Wilber force came together and helped them renovate the garage into a living room by putting up wallboard, installing windows, painting, and reflooring. It needed to be done and we did it. By pooling our few talents and those of a carpenter friend of Beau's, we finished in a week.

Even without a big project the family all pitch in. The big ones hold on to the little ones in the water, give them rides on the fire engine, read to them, and in return get big sloppy kisses and adoration.

This mindset creates a great deal of confidence, allowing our children to see that they can do, and be a success at, whatever they want.

Beau's Best Banana Bread

Beau was a funny little boy who went his own way in thought and deed. Always cheerful, but not always happy, one day I caught him in a pensive mood at about age eight. I asked what he was thinking about. He told me "it was hard being me." He had decided that his only solution was to wait until his friends grew up.

So I thought and thought what we could do to give Beau projects all of his own with some name recognition. As he loved to cook I asked him the next day if he would just follow the recipe in the cookbook for banana bread. Then we hunted around for something to add that would make it his own. Walnuts. The bread was delicious and it was gone in one sitting and declared by all to be "Beau's Best Banana Bread," and from then on it was always requested by name.

Soon after that his invitation to visit his friend Mack fell through and Beau was crushed. I knew in the scheme of things this was more devastating than he let on. So I asked Beau if he would like to go on an adventure with me.

It was second best but we could make a really interesting trip of it. So we planned to take a drive for a week up to North Carolina to pick up Ashley and Van at summer camp. The catch was, I would do the driving, and he would do the navigating. Beau pored over that map and by the time we got in the car with all his lists and maps we had a pretty good plan. It was early August and the AC didn't work in the car so every fifty miles Beau would say, "Time for dip!" I'd pull over and he would go for a refreshing swim. We went everywhere in his T-shirt, bathing suit, and flip-flops: Alligator Land, Busch Gardens, NASA, several forgettable places and then headed for Hilton Head where Beau had planned three days.

By the time we drew up outside a big glassy hotel we were a wreck! The concierge asked what in the world we wanted. We said we wanted a room. He said archly, "Madam, the least expensive room here is seventy-nine dollars per night." "Great," I perked up, "we'll stay here!" He advised that it was pay in advance so I flashed him my platinum card and asked for the little fridge to be stocked with "diet cokes, champagne, and candy bars, and if anyone asked, we were at the pool!"

We drove off to Columbia, Georgia, to have a look at the governor's mansion as our house in Greenwich was supposed to be a copy of it. Glory, it was a long way to the capital. Once there we followed signs, and if memory serves, the governor's mansion was about half the size of ours and made of white painted brick. We frankly felt like imposters. We asked at the gate if this were the governor's mansion from years ago. We thought it would look more like a . . . well, a plantation house. "Oh yes," the old gentleman agreed, "it once did before it was Shermanized."

Steve's Perspective

Supplemental Education

When the children graduated from preparatory school, we wanted each of them in turn to experience a real challenge where they would have to rely substantially on themselves. We felt that would help them appreciate education and learn some home truths.

Both Stevie and I had taken time to finish schooling. She left Rollins College after one year and worked at banks while doing charity work, but resumed studies after a couple of years by attending a community college and eventually graduating from Florida Southern. I left Yale after two years, worked five years for a nonprofit organization and then was drafted into the army. Five years later I returned to academe and earned an MBA degree from Columbia. Both of us had been among the youngest in our classes, and we felt retrospectively that we should have taken a year off to learn about the world (a euphemism for grow up).

The deal we put to the children was this: Consider taking a gap year (as they call this in England where it is a fairly common practice). We will support you financially if you come up with a sensible and interesting program and can explain it well.

Otherwise, we'll help you find a summer job of an eleemosynary nature, where we will pay you your college spending money at the end. We will pay minimum wage times an assumed forty-hour week, times the number of weeks worked, with only one string attached. You will have to write a paper explaining what you did, what you had learned, and why it was important.

All three of them declined the gap year, but had summer programs that significantly affected them.

Van agreed to take a summer job at Camp Xaxaba (the "x" pronounced with a clicking tongue if you could learn how, KeeKaaBa if you couldn't do it right.) Xaxaba is on an island in the Okavango Delta in the heart of Botswana, due north of South Africa and substantially covered by the Kalahari Desert. The rains from mountain ranges in Angola wash down as a great river into the Kalahari, creating a huge inland delta. The water lies in extended lakes for some of the year, imprisoning all manner of animal life except big cats who do not like water or small islands. Some of the water disappears underground but most eventually evaporates, at which time animals migrate in and out of the area.

We had confidence in the opportunity because a good friend of ours, Lord Bill Coleridge, had placed his son there for a few months, and he had profited from the experience. Our family went together to Xaxaba as tourists, gliding on macorros (hollowed-out log canoes) through the tall grasses past crocodiles on the banks, and, on the islands, small herds of giraffe and antelope. We flew off in the bush planes to climb rocks and look at prehistoric wall paintings by the Khoi people, whose descendants still lived in the Kalahari. (Many will remember that wonderful movie *The Gods Must be Crazy,* which starred some of these bushmen.)

Then we left Van in the care of Kennedy, a very large and powerfully built black man who was the camp manager, and set off on further adventures. Van stayed, as assistant camp manager and bartender.

Van's paper about the summer was fascinating. His favorite activity was going in the evenings down to the local village, where he and Kennedy would drink beer with the locals and just talk in Pidgin English. He learned from Kennedy in many ways, but on one occasion he forgot to lock up one of the bars and in the morning there was no more beer or booze there. His pay from the camp was docked the entire amount. He didn't forget again. Most importantly he learned to read the mood of a place or the people there. Africa is so beautiful, yet can turn ugly so quickly. Kennedy was not a member of the local tribe and had to be very careful in the village where he was nearly a king by virtue of the money the camp spent locally. So he was affably charming in the local bush bar until it became time to leave, sometimes in a hurry.

Van's summer work led to him specializing in Africa in the U.S. Department of State, including five years living in West Africa, and building his career on country analysis and security.

Ashley had her turn two years later, in 1990, just as the Berlin Wall was coming down and the Soviet empire was collapsing. A nearby neighbor up Hillside Road in Greenwich had escaped from Czechoslovakia as a child and was looking for ways to help the country emerge from communism and the cold war privations. He came from Bratislava, the capital of the Slovak part of the country, which soon split off from the Czechs to become the Slovak Republic. Bratislava was only a couple of hours drive from Vienna, which we all knew well.

At our neighbors' home we met a politician from the Christian Democratic Party (KDH) who wanted to develop an English-language training program to help integrate their citizenry back into Europe. All the necessary teaching materials and logistical backup would be there and they would arrange housing, etc. We had a family meeting on this one, and decided it would be a good project, and that while it would remain Ashley's project, Van would go along as well. Our decorator's daughter went along too.

Well, nothing was as promised or expected. They were met at the airport and transported to the KDH headquarters, but nothing was in place: no meeting hall, no books, no schedule, no nothing. The hosts found a spare flat in nearby Petrzalka, across the Danube River from Bratislava, but it was in a Soviet-built blocks of flats that are commonly called instant slums. The fourth-floor flat was a walk-up as the elevators didn't work, the water sometimes worked, and chunks of concrete fell off the building from time to time.

The kids got to work right away and handed out flyers announcing the new English courses at the KDH headquarters building. They pressured the party to get books right away. People started coming and the enthusiasm of these young untrained teachers was addictive. An ad was run in the local newspaper and hundreds swamped in. Eventually they got their books and teaching aids, and the program continued to be fueled by local hunger for English. When our trio returned in early September to get to college, they were replaced by thirteen fully trained and experienced teachers from England who were sponsored by a development grant from a government agency.

Ashley's paper described all the circumstances and the heartwarming satisfaction of meeting the voracious hunger for the ideas and knowledge of the free world. But our children experienced firsthand the horrific effects of the communist system, in physical as well as mental terms. Ashley's students asked her "What is opinion?" "What is making up your mind?" And it was a thunderous awakening to her that these people had never decided anything; it had been decided for them. She said that slowly, slowly she got the idea across by starting small: "Every morning you go to your closet and decide, 'Do I wear the red shirt or the blue shirt?' That is making up your mind."

Her students, from peach pickers to movie stars, were kind and generous to a fault. Most days they spent their entire time looking for food to buy. Often their students invited them home to what appeared to be collapsing houses but once inside were filled with treasures—beautiful paintings and porcelains, silver and metal work, ancient family bibles and eighteenth-century furniture, and food they never saw on any grocery shelf. Other students took them to the mountains on weekends to hike and picnic. There were never any better hosts.

Two years later, in 1992, it was Beau's turn. Stevie had lined up a position for him in Madagascar working with a research team studying the many kinds of lemurs there. A couple of months before he was due to go, there was a revolution in Madagascar and the State Department advised citizens not to go there. So Beau found his own project.

While crossing campus at a school he was visiting to decide where to go to college, he came across a professor doing Tai Chi exercises. Beau stopped to chat with him and wound up working for a project with which the professor was involved at the Tibetan University in Exile in southern India.

The job was to teach conversational English to the young Tibetan monks in training. While he taught them English, they taught him their ways. The university was intentionally and truly isolated. The Indians had enough trouble with the Chinese along their roof-of-the-world border that they did not wish to be accused of providing a safe haven for terrorists or to be in any way seen as promoting anything other than humanitarian ends. It was in the middle of the country in Karnataka State where there weren't even any telephones.

Beau had to take a tuk tuk (a small motorized three-wheeled taxi) ride of half an hour to get to a telephone. He lived in the dormitory with his students, and learned from them while they learned from him. Their happiness living in a world of almost complete privation by American standards, away from their native land, home, and families for the most part, deeply impressed him. And the sights, smells, and tastes of India are hard to get out of your system.

Beau later started an Internet-based business to wholesale and retail all-natural cotton vegetable-dyed Indian tapestries. He ran this for some eight years and traveled to India on purchasing trips where he visited us (by that time we were living in Mumbai).

An occasional refresher course from Hard Knocks University is a great education, and should be sought periodically.

SIX

What We Learn
from the Animals

Respecting personal space

ur second Niger team met us at our hotel at Niger's border in the morning after the highly eventful international border crossing across the Niger River (discussed on pages 76–77), and a two-rutted dirt road with two felled trees marking the line. Breakfast was, as always, served in the garden that was also occupied with the funniest looking bustards, almost too big to be birds, but not to be questioned. They wanted our baguettes and aggressively reminded us with every bite we took. The terrace overlooked the river, which at that time of day had busy traffic as folks went to work. Great pods of hippos lived in the same space. One hippo launched his huge frame out of the water at a passing boat and thankfully only swamped it. What a way to start the day! We surmised that we would be challenged at every turn in the road in this new country of Niger.

We drove to the beach along the river and took a boat to the "Bird Island" where Steve clocked five new birds. We had lots of bailing to do in our leaky vessel. We encountered no hippos, thankfully. We returned to the shore and the long empty beach, and our guide indicated that we should put in "Just Here."

A woman brought her laundry, dishes, and water bottles, and our guide thoughtlessly entered her space. I was indignant and told the local guide that we should move out of her way. He shrugged. At which point the local woman understood my anger and joined in, angry herself at being marginalized, and we two sisters did a routine, happily in unison—a small conquest—but we looked a "high five" at each other and in that moment continents melted into a momentary unison of sisterhood.

It was a morning's drive to the lovely colonial town of Niamey and the Grand Hotel with its busy rooftop restaurant, which was where all expats gathered from every hotel and apartment. The views from the top floor across the Niger and the beautiful sunsets were refreshingly comfortable. Only now did we realize how deep we have been in the third world.

They start out small and cute . . .

If you ask anyone about Uganda, most will say it was ruled by Idi Amin, the harsh and hated dictator who lived in exile in Saudi Arabia for thirty years before dying a few years ago. Uganda's northern border with the Sudan is problematic because insurgents dwell on both sides of the border; Sudanese sneak into exile there, and it is a terrible situation.

Despite all of this, our visit to Uganda was one of the most fascinating trips we've ever made. The equator runs through Uganda, a little further south than Jinja. Jinja is on the northern shore of Lake Victoria, the source of the Nile. Uganda is home to many different animals, providing extensive photo safaris. The bird life is truly amazing and Johnny Weissmuller made his Tarzan movies in a park in Kampala. Bill Clinton visited here in 1998 and as a result there are many evening spots called "Monica Lewinsky's Joint."

The history of the white man in Africa was dominated for three centuries by the search for the source of the Nile, which is the north side of Lake Victoria—the huge lake between Uganda and Tanzania. The American adventurer Stanley had many tribulations; such swirls and swells of water are hard to imagine in Africa. I've never seen water so plentiful. The many Niles dominate the Ugandan landscape, not the least of which is the White Nile that feeds Murchison Falls in the northwest. Now our destination was to be Murchison National Park via the ubiquitous red clay roads. Usually after the colonialists left a country it wasn't long before national pride caused local name changes that reflect the name to local dialect. Our guide explained that the Ugandan name for Murchison Falls was Kabalega, named by Idi Amin. But because the citizens wanted to wipe out any evidence of Idi, they changed back to calling it Murchison, the head of the Royal Geographical Society when it was discovered.

Our safari lodge looked rundown from the outside, perched upon the escarpment overlooking the river. But inside it was beautiful, with Ralph Lauren steamer trunks for decoration. Just below the lodge was the guides' camp. The guides led safaris in peacetime, but toted AK-47s and were trained in warfare.

One little hippo was munching on the grass between the houses. We were surprised to find a hippo out of the water at this time of day, and our guide explained that this little fellow challenged the dominant male of the pod and was thrown out. They called him Oswald, and they knew he was theirs for another five years until he was big enough to challenge the dominant male again.

One sleepless night I got up and changed into my bathing suit to have a dip to cool off when a loud "kerplunk" came from the pool. I looked out but there was little light and one could make out a dark form in the pool. I woke Steve to come with me while I had a dip. He rubbed the sleep out of his eyes and announced that Oswald had beaten me to it! I wasn't going in there! We watched our hippo do everything but ballet in the growing light until he got out and trotted down the hill. The staff was so mad at Oswald the next morning. Oswald had left a terrible mess at the bottom that disintegrated every time it was approached by shovel. So began four days of draining, scrubbing, and refilling the pool.

Animals know our soft spots

In Nairobi we stayed at the New Stanley hotel. The bar was a microcosm of the population of Kenya. Several old boys in tan, plus fours

Stevie craning to watch a pair of lions, Tanzania, 2004.

and argyle socks, and lots of facial hair toast the moment. Two Masai warriors greet each other wrapped in red blankets and carrying staffs, their ears pierced so widely that film canisters could fit in the holes. Life as usual at the Stanley.

What was new was as you left the hotel the doorman barks, "Earrings, Madam!"—your sign to take them off due to the bad element in Nairobi streets. Security guards with AK-47s, however, dot the way around the block to protect the businesses and the shoppers.

We had a delicious treat while staying at Giraffe Manor, an English-country house turned into a hotel at the edge of Nairobi. Free-ranging Rothschild Giraffe gracefully roamed the gardens and came for a look through the windows at breakfast, which were opened to allow the guests to feed the giraffes a sort of kibble. The giraffes can just see into the second-floor rooms so they find you there for another top-up! From this room across the lawns and into the distance we enjoyed a magnificent view of Mt. Kilimanjaro.

Size matters . . . sort of

Mother and I were ambling toward the canoes to remove the last of our goods before the rest continued on the croc/hippo safari. We were practicing not facing away from the river, which the crocodiles interpreted as an open invitation. Instead we hear thundering hoof beats approaching from the rear and turned in surprise to see a giant elephant chasing us out on the strip of land.

Dale, our guide told us, *"Stop! Face the elephant and draw big ears!"*

We had no idea what any of that meant, but Dale raced ahead of us. He drew elephant ears in the air and yelled in his deepest baritone, *"Stop!"* The elephant was like a cartoon character bracing to a stop with giant puffs of smoke coming out from behind his heels. He put his head down and wandered away with what seemed like contriteness.

The elephant knows he is a big animal and uses his size to intimidate, but he is really a jelly bean. Don't you know folks like this?

Human versus Animal

We had just deplaned from Singapore in Port Morseby, Papua New Guinea, and were put on a little twenty-seater bus that was soon out of town and immediately in deep rural countryside. The idea was for us to have our picnic lunch along the river. We arrived in time, however, to see loin-clothed warriors throwing spears across the river at some non-warriors with a crocodile tied up in vegetation. We beat a path to safety whilst our local guide weighed in to find out what was going on. He came just in time to negotiate a diplomatic solution. The tribe with the spears had caught another tribe stealing their river's crocodile.

Every river has a god in the form of a crocodile. So much recent poaching (they are delicious) had reduced the croc population to one. So it truly was the only croc around.

We seemed to go from one village war to another. The burning drove the birds high into the mountains to the tops of trees. So we had little to share with our birding friends at the end of the trip. We were taken by a cockroach-infested small plane over the mountains to a beautiful but empty lodge for a few days in hopes the bird population would be stable on this side. The pilot circled and circled and finally came on the speaker, "Would everyone look out the windows: there is a landing strip down there somewhere!" Another twenty minutes of crossed fingers and sweaty brows got us to the destination.

More like us than we'd like to admit

Monkeys are allowed to run loose in almost every town in India. They travel in groups foraging for fruit and nuts. They are hilarious, seeing something new they find a high place to sit and watch these funny humans perform. They are observers and witnesses and chatterboxes.

Many books written in India figure the monkeys into their stories. My favorite is *Hullabaloo in the Guava Orchard,* by Kiran Desai. When all else fails they blame it on the monkeys. A word of warning: Don't ever look a monkey in the eye. He will become infuriated. I soon got it that the Indians took us foreigners to be like monkeys: watching their funny ways, chattering and not liking it one bit when examined too closely. That helped me understand their lack of need for us and brought me to an appropriate level of importance, or should I say irrelevance.

Nature at its most basic

For Steve's sixtieth birthday we decided to go on a mega bird-watching trip, down to the South pole. We chose the Holland-America cruise line due to its leisurely schedule and the stability of its larger ships operating in the often hellishly rough waters south of the Straits of Magellan and the Drake Passage. I have cast-iron plumbing and never get seasick, while Steve wears wristbands that keep him steady on the roughest days.

We started out in Rio and from there sailed on the *MS Ryndam* to Buenos Aires, Montevideo, on to the Falkland Islands (the Malvinas according to the Argentines) and then Ushuaia, Argentina, the southernmost city on the continent. One felt a gold-rush mentality, with saloons and souvenir shops wall to wall along the main street. It was the Wild West moved south.

When we sailed from Ushuaia, nature was the overwhelming force, with very little evidence of human activity. Around us, nature was all-absorbing. The extreme harshness of the environment (blinding sleet in gale-force winds, the boat rocking and pitching, nothing to be seen on the horizon except wandering albatross and storm petrels, and for that matter no visible horizon) made the occasional rays of sunshine breaking through or the majestic rocky spike pinnacles of Elephant Island all the more beautiful.

One day in the Murdo Sound the sun came out gloriously and the pace of glacier melt seemed to speed up. There were fragments of icebergs ("bergie-bits") everywhere and our pace slowed to watch for large chunks better avoided by the helmsman. We saw a wave of many hundreds of emperor penguins surfing as if one body, rising and falling in measured cadence the way a dolphin swims. The black backs of the penguins alternated with flashes of white as they occasionally changed direction, revealing white underbellies, all done at amazing speed (as if they were being chased by sea lions) and in unison with such precision that you felt one mind had to be controlling this. All the deck railings on the port side were lined two or three deep by people standing silently, gape-mouthed in awe, nobody daring to speak lest we somehow break the magic spell of the penguins.

The next day we came alongside an abandoned Argentinean meteorological station. One of the buildings was a metal Quonset hut, quite a large shed, perhaps thirty feet long, with the doors swung wide open at the end facing the water. The captain explained over the intercom that the dominant sea lion liked to crawl up the ice bank to the shed and roar his challenge to any other males to keep them away from his herd of females. The amplification of his voice by the man-made echo chamber would obviously convince many aspiring rivals that this was truly a huge sea lion, and not worth challenging. The next day as we sailed slowly by in the opposite direction heading back toward Chile, we heard a truly awful din coming from the shed. The big boy had taken up residence.

As we sailed up the Drake Passage within Chilean waters, the ship passed a low, flat rock perhaps fifty yards long and ten yards wide. The ship slowed because the islet was covered by penguins, cormorants, and seals—literally covered. There seemed to be no room left for one more of anything. Then we saw the brilliant black and white of two orcas (killer whales), seemingly mother and child, breaking the surface, skimming by and waiting for someone on the island to get hungry and leave the refuge. We stood dead in the water for a while and the fearsome anticipation we could feel emanating from the island was remarkable. We almost expected the least popular to get "voted off the island" as they all would soon have to find food, but all sat silent in a true silence of the lambs.

We saw on this trip nature, up close. It was so basic, at times beautiful or ugly, but always awe inspiring.

For the birds

It has always puzzled me that so many people find birds unfulfilling pets. My first, last, and favorite creature was a bird: Aiwa, the African Gray, who came to live with us soon after our move to Dir'aiyah. Each morning the staff, Iman, came into the house to start his day, greeted Aiwa on his cage in the breakfast room and then went to the kitchen for breakfast. Iman always stood formally in front of his cage, bowed and greeted him. Aiwa mimicked the greeting including the deep bow. Adam, our fantastic weight-lifting Somali driver, came through with the African equivalent of "Yo, Aiwa," which he repeated with the same jaunty air.

But Aiwa was my bird. He expected a cuddle and some sweet meows before breakfast. He considered the most interesting of the household to be Ashley and Beau. He loved to hear the two of them argue, laugh their musical laughs at the unknown, make paper airplanes to dive bomb each other and Aiwa. And Ashley had that trumpet that Aiwa spent every unoccupied minute trying to mimic.

As soon as they were out the door Aiwa would clear his voice and work on the new vocabulary from the morning. My desk was one hundred feet down the narrow room that served many functions. During one stage I was writing my book on the Dir'aiyah ruins and had a self-imposed deadline. Aiwa had endured days of being ignored all morning. From the corner of my eye I watched him slide down the table leg and make his pigeon-toed way along the long path leading toward my desk. When he arrived I thought I would just finish the sentence before playing with him.

But Aiwa wasn't waiting that long. He looked up at me and said, "You want to sit on my shoulder?" He spent the rest of the morning rearranging paper clips and mimicking my laugh on the telephone.

When we moved into Riyadh we worried that he had parasites because the vet tried every other form of cure, including trying to give him a shot with a hypodermic needle that was scary big. Aiwa left my arms and waddled, stiff legged, around the table, and if he could, he would have put his hands on his hips in indignation. "Don't do that," he accused, "stop messing with me!"

Finally, we called it an iron lung: a cuff of photo paper taped in a cone over his head so he couldn't pull out his feathers. He sat stock-still for two days and finally began to move around. But it did the trick . . . Aiwa was just over-engaged.

One day our cat jumped in the cage to eat the chicken bones our cook, Rosemary, put in for him. I walked in on this scene and the cat knew he wasn't supposed to be there and leapt out. We learned in our menagerie that in the animal kingdom one family never eats another. So when the cat found the nest of mice, she spent the morning purring and cuddling them. These are good lessons for human families too!

Intuition

Beau and his family went camping by a river in Sedona and their dog,

Raven, took sick. They drove into town and found a vet where Suki and the boys took Raven. Beau sat on a bench down the street under a tree. Soon a woman came out of a crystal shop and sat down to light up. Raven and the gang soon came out of the vet's. Raven looked down the street at the woman next to Beau. The woman turned to Beau and asked, "Is that your dog?" "Why, yes it is," he said with some surprise. She then continued, "Your dog tells me she is pretty and her name is Raven and that she drank too much river water and doesn't feel well."

Suki and the boys came out and announced the vet's opinion. You could have knocked Beau over with a feather.

Ashley and Olivier's wedding in Sarasota, Florida, April 14, 2002.

Clockwise from top left: Kathy Wilberding (Steve's mother), Olivier Balavoine, Ashley Balavoine, Ann Spaulding (Onnie), Stevie, Steve.

Beau, flanked by Steve and Stevie, at his graduation from Thunderbird, August 2005.

SEVEN

We Are Family

The house does not rest upon the ground,
but upon a woman.

–Mexican proverb

So much of my life has been about my family, that I'm really not sure where to begin this chapter. I love them dearly, and making sure we had a solid and stable family life, even while relocating every few years, influenced many, perhaps nearly all, of my decisions. Yet I never knew if I was doing the right thing. You can read books on what to bring and what you'll find, but you'll never read a word about being alienated by your own people in a foreign country thousands of miles from home or how do you get through the next 254 days before you can go home again. My mother-in-law once said to me, "I am not jealous of you." In utter surprise I said, "Jealous!?! Who would be jealous of this? It is darn hard work."

Relocating

Putting the children first resulted in a strategy I developed further each time we moved. First and foremost was helping them look a part of their new culture. It is a reality that too often we judge—and are judged—based on appearance. Fighting against that truth when moving from place to place as often as we did, when our children were

Stevie and her brood, Keene, New York, July 2004.

constantly the new kids on the block, would have been beyond futile. It would have been downright unfair to them.

Accepting the reality that we all would be judged by our appearances, I would take the children down to the main thoroughfare or shopping center and we would people watch. We'd make a game of all we needed to get to have them fit in. "Oh, Ashley. You'll need at least twenty skirts just like that, won't you?" And then we'd both laugh, knowing this was ridiculous. The boys and I would do the same.

The next step would be to help them make friends quickly so they would not be lonely, and I do think the first step helped a great deal with the second. Right or wrong, it wasn't my decision. I wasn't out to change the world; I just wanted happy and well-adjusted children.

The quest for new friends meant that we would invite the new chums over as soon as we could, even if it meant entertaining them in our hotel room. The upshot of this was that I quickly met their parents that way and thus was able to develop my own circle of friends as well.

Next would be getting them involved in the activities they had previously pursued, or helping them explore new ones offered by our new society. In Japan, for example, Van became quite taken with the Japanese opera, the Kabuki. He was so enthralled in fact that he'd dress in pajamas at home and act like a superhero opera star. He had the sounds and motions down to perfection.

We went every week, and it soon became apparent to the ticket sellers that Van was the Kabuki fan. So they worked it out that we would pay the price of the ticket in the stars and they would give him the hanamichi seats, the seats in the coveted runway stretching from the stage to the back of the theater. He knew (at age four) how to wave down a taxi, ask for the Kabuki theater, buy a ticket, and knew his way around the theater of five levels with food sales on each wing, since the whole performance lasted five hours or more.

Ashley did ballet at an old institution, as well as piano. She lumbered through figure skating at Lady Eden's School in London (those skates were one of five pairs of shoes she needed for school). Beau played rounders and cricket at his school. Both the boys did beagling and tennis on weekends. Most of these I had no ideas about: the rules, the uniforms, etc.

Tokyo, Japan, 1975.

Onnie's Perspective

I was amazed at how quickly Stevie could put a house together. The way my daughter teams up with those working with her is remarkable, too. For example, Henry, her driver in India, knew to circle the block two times and Stevie would be finished with a particular errand. She helps make those who work with her better at their jobs; she makes them complicit in her plans. Stevie makes them important to her, expects them to do their best.

How to make friends no matter where you are

After getting the children settled into a basically functional routine, I discovered a pattern that seemed to work well for establishing the next level of connection to our new home.

I'd make sure we found a good church. This gave us an instant community of people who, at least at some level, had a connection with us.

I would make sure to celebrate the culture where we were, and I talk about different holidays and ceremonies in more detail in other parts of this book.

Adirondacks, Summer, 1989.

Hanna Brown Wilberding's Baptism, Venice, Florida, 1999.

We would start collecting art and other cultural items of the country we were in. This allowed me to meet other English-speaking collectors, and to get to know the collectors who are natives in the country. My first collection, put together in Japan, was Ming blue-and-white fourteenth to sixteenth century porcelain, and I still have the first piece I ever owned.

In Japan I collected Ming, Japanese Ukioy-e, wood block etchings, Imari porcelain. In England, it was English furniture, some silver, Chippendale furniture, and seventeenth-century oak furniture, paintings, and pot lids. (The lids of important pieces whose base was lost or broken, like a teapot or sugar bowl. I couldn't afford the whole pot so I delighted myself with a study collection of the pot lids.) In Saudi Arabia I was on a quest for silk carpets and Turkoman jewelry. And I enjoyed paintings throughout the world, but especially the modern work of India.

In most places I was fascinated by how crafts intermingle; in Turkoman jewelry, for example, the jewelry reflected the same detail or iconography as the silk rugs. Getting to know the art of a culture is one of the best ways to get to know the people, and I talk about all of this in more detail in other parts of this book.

In looking for friends in each new place, I also quickly learned how to determine which friends to keep close, and which not to. The basic rule while living overseas (and you could argue it ought to be the rule everywhere) is that you can do anything but complain.

Stevie enjoying live music by Beau's rock band on her porch, Casey Key, Florida, September 2008.

I learned to share my friends; some had a different philosophy since good, solid friends could be hard to come by. But I learned that my good, solid friends had other good, solid friends, so I would host a party every autumn where everyone met and mingled. Even now people will say, "I met so-and-so at your coffee in Tokyo thirty-five years ago."

A Friend's Perspective

Sarah Searight

People often talk about neighbors and neighborliness and so on and so forth. But to arrive in a strange country, strange city, strange house and find a *real neighbor* was the most amazing experience. This was 1974 and the Lushes were moving into Roppongi in the heart of Tokyo with a four-year-old and a six-year-old and lo and behold, there was another four-year-old right next door, with a mother and a father (and smaller siblings) barely twenty yards away. I have to say Stevie's burden was worse than mine because her eldest, Van, was the four year old; Ashley and Beau were a lot smaller, so that dreaded 5 P.M. hour needed brightening, and that was where neighborliness began. And Van and Cosmo became good friends; Cosmo even ushered many years later at Van's wedding.

Thereafter we followed each other around the world for several years. The Wilberdings came to London—not quite neighbors as they were the wrong side of the river—but plenty of childish escapades for Van and Cosmo. Then my Julian moved to Abu Dhabi and Steve to Riyadh; I had the good fortune to visit them in Dir'aiyah, that wonderful farmhouse; Stevie organized a party the evening of my arrival, with gallons of deliciously fizzy wine, which her guests were extraordinarily rude about. Years later we found them not long in Bombay but their apartment already filling with splendid contemporary Indian art. And then Greenwich, and then Florida where my ailing Julian relaxed in the cottage by the ocean before heading for Amazonia.

Stevie has been the staunchest, wittiest of friends; we are blessed to know her and her entire family.

India was the one spot where my normal strategy did not play out as usual. Part of the issue was that I didn't have my usual props—the children and their activities. But it went beyond that somehow, and I couldn't seem to crack the code to befriending the wives and families of Steve's coworkers there. I did, though, make lovely friends in the cultural groups I was in, and with artists and neighbors.

Indians sometimes seemed to look at foreigners as though they were showing off their foreignness, and this attitude spurred me to work to rejuvenate the American Women's Club and help a new group of young women there. As hard as it was on me after my years of living abroad, I had real empathy for the young women just starting out who were flummoxed by the place and their families' roles in it.

End product

I have always aimed to turn out a good end product. I have wanted my children to be solid, happy, productive citizens who were bold and brave and thought independently. I have wanted them to have the confidence to achieve whatever they wanted to achieve, even if it was out of the ordinary or not something I would have chosen for them. I talk about confidence elsewhere in this book, too. I have encouraged them to find the freedom to make informed decisions, even if those decisions were not ones I would have made.

Consequently, I gave them a lot, both emotionally and in terms of material things, but I also expected a great deal from them too. I was very strict about good manners and having them finish what they started. My children earned what they enjoyed and rose to meet some very high expectations indeed.

Beau's Perspective

Mom's expectations of us extended to our friends as well. Really, to all of humanity, but that's another topic. One afternoon, she shamed Piers Curry, age twenty-five, my great old friend and business partner of many years, utterly and completely. That moment goes down as one of the funniest and greatest Mom moments among my friends.

Piers had bought a vintage VW Karmann Ghia. It was his pride and joy. He buzzed around town until one afternoon it caught fire on the highway. I was in the car when that happened; the incident was hysterically funny, and we were both fine. The car was instantly a burned-out hulk, and I knew that Piers was both miserable and without a place to park it, I offered my driveway as a temporary spot for his ride. He gladly accepted.

Mom came by the house a month later to discover the mess still in my driveway.

"What's this?" she asked.

"That is Piers' car. He's storing it here until he can fix it," I replied.

"Where's Piers?"

"At work."

"Let's go say hi," she said.

"Fine," I said. "Just please don't mention the car because he is under a lot of stress right now."

"Don't worry, I won't say a thing."

We drove over, and before we walked in I said it again. "Please don't talk about the car, Mom."

Again, she chided me for my persistence.

As we walked in, Piers sees Mom and strides over, smiling, saying, "Matriarch! How are you?"

Mom freezes him with a single outstretched index finger. With a face full of fury, she roared, *"Shame! Shaaame!"*

Piers' face couldn't have fallen further. Trapped and speechless, he stood there, transfixed, as Mom lit into him. She told him he'd better have AAA on the phone inside ten seconds or his ass was grass. In three seconds, he was speaking to an operator and asking me for a ride to my home.

The car was gone forty-five minutes after Mom saw it in my driveway.

Piers has always loved my mom. Nothing can change that. But if you want to get a laugh in our social circle, all you have to do is extend your index finger and shout, "Shame!"

Our high expectations of our children extended beyond good grades in school and fulfilling their own social and work obligations to helping us fulfill ours as well. The reality of our life was that we entertained a wide array of foreign and U.S. business people, diplomats, and artists, and because we did that in our home, we had one of two choices. Either send our children away during events, or instill in them at an early age what was expected of them at the party. I believed they would be served better long term by knowing how to conduct themselves in a variety of situations, so I took that (always challenging) route.

It was not enough for them to be seen and not heard at our gatherings. I expected them to be able to carry on a conversation with whomever they were seated next to. This, of course, led to some interesting conversations, including the time a matriarch of our social circle complimented me on Beau's social skills. Curious, I asked what they had spoken about. "Skateboards," she replied.

It turned out that Beau had politely engaged her in a conversation about whether she had ever skateboarded, and then proceeded to share, in a charming fashion, all types of skateboarding information with this seventy-year-old woman wearing pearls.

Beau's Perspective

Mom has always been a highly involved and protective parent, and she was over the top on a lot of things. She gave us a chance to develop not only academically, but artistically and athletically as well. Ashley took trumpet and piano; Van the cornet and piano; and I learned piano, trombone, and drums.

The piano and trombone were hurdles on the way to drumming. I was always a drummer. This was Mom's burden, and she bore it willingly. In high school, Mom defended my right to play drums against our entire neighborhood. Mom always said that when you live with a drummer you realize every surface becomes a drum head, from lead crystal vases to Jacuzzis.

I had a band called Kozmic Blooze, and we were *loud*. We covered bands like Santana, Otis Redding, and the Allman Brothers Band. Mom loved the fact that we were creating something. She trusted us and gave us the kind of autonomy that only gets given the youngest sibling in large families. In three years of three-a-week practices, she never once came up to interrupt our practices, even when parents called wanting to speak with their son. She always said, "I never interrupt but you are welcome to come over and make that decision." Some of our original songs were antisocial at best, but it didn't matter. We were inspired, and Mom knew it.

She may not have liked our music, but she was damn well going to support it.

She may not have liked it, but she listened for elements she could appreciate.

She dealt with the noise and treated the members of my band like her own children. They loved her and feared her, a lot like I did (and still perhaps do in some ways!). All of my friends see her in that way, as a sort of matriarch. She is someone to share your best stories, proudest accomplishments, and biggest dreams with. You want to hide the ugly stuff, though.

Her support of our band harkens back to a book called *Just Look,* which Mom read to me as a child. There were hidden pictures among the pictures: sort of visual riddles. Art and music were bedfellows for Mom, so it didn't matter what we were doing, as long as we were creating something, and *Just Look* was part of her way of cultivating a love of creativity in us at an early age.

Mom will tell you that great art has always required great sacrifice, and sacrifice she did, at least her ears (and those of our neighbors!) during my high school years.

Know when to hold 'em, know when to fold 'em

Conscious compromise was always a critical element in how I managed our days, whether we were at home or out on an adventure exploring a new activity, area of town, or market. For example, when traveling, we had a family agreement to eat at a McDonald's once during the trip. How did we find our "grease fix"? Ashley, who is now a professional "nose"—a creator of perfumes and other scents—used to sniff them out for us!

Had she been in India with us when we later landed there, it would have been interesting to see if her nose would have been as effective. There, they served Maharaja Macs, made of lamb instead of beef due to the sacredness of cows. And they were good! They were also a half hour away from our house!

At certain times, though, we never compromised. When we told the children to stop bickering in the car or we'd walk, we meant it. We weren't bluffing. Steve and I pulled the car over on several occasions, with Steve getting out and walking with the three children home—even if it were several miles away, raining, foggy, or any of the rest of the array of weather we faced during our travels. As a parent, never, ever threaten something you won't follow through on. You'll lose all credibility. And never argue with a child.

Connection with each other

As a result of our frequent moves, I believe our children were closer to each other and formed tighter bonds with one another than other siblings. While other children in other countries might be off going to the movies with their friends, ours sat around watching *Blazing Saddles* again and again (we owned only six videos at first); memorizing the lines in what I'm certain was a deliberate plan to torment us with continuing renditions of the dialogue in years to come. Their "theater" was a tent in our oasis palace-farm in Saudi Arabia, with a red velvet ceiling, Iranian tribal rugs on the walls, cushions around the borders, and the occasional scorpion that came in to watch, too.

How you can use this

The regular family dinner has become a cliché, but it is exactly that sort of commitment to regular family functions that will give your kids a good foundation and a sense of stability. Give a lot and expect a lot, and setting aside regular family time is a good example of this. If you are willing to give your children time, then you can reasonably expect them to give their time in return.

If you don't have children, or they are grown, you and your partner will still benefit from set-aside shared time, whether it's dining together, game night, movie night, or long walks together. The commitment to regular time together is a key building block in any relationship.

Ultimately, what is important to you? How you choose to spend your time should reflect that. Any compromise on how you spend your time, what you expect from your family, and what they expect from you should be done with intention, not just as a Band-Aid to patch up a bad moment.

Relocation Cheat Sheet

1. Get used to the appearances of others, and develop an understanding and attitude about them. Overly cynical attitudes will undermine any learning your family will have the occasion to do.

2. Work to build a network of friends for your kids first. The network will hopefully include a number of parents who are good fun. My networks came mostly through my kids, church and church-related activities, my collections and our many parties mixing new and old friends.

3. Find threads of continuity for your children. For us, we found similar activities in new places. Soccer was a good one for the boys. I find that if you can give kids some continuity, they can take on new activities with grace.

4. Most importantly, trust in the flexibility of your kids. They will figure their moving challenges out, but *make sure that you are there for them.*

EIGHT

Growing into Death

I am comfortable with death, and now I want to make my family comfortable as well. We embarked upon early discussions and continue to do so as I fight my battle with cancer. My children aren't selfish in their responses, just afraid, and they don't know life without me. They want me well, and are trying their best to get me that way again. Beau is more conversant with death because of his classes at college. The miracles of modern education amaze me sometimes.

From left: Steve, Van, Stevie, Beau, and Ashley on Casey Key,
a week after Stevie's cancer diagnosis, April 2007.

I'm taking their comments and trying to find ways to bring comfort. "Don't Die." If it were only as simple as that! I am helping my daughter find alternatives to me after I am gone, but I know this takes the nurturing of time. I have started by giving things of meaning to each of them—jewelry, artwork, travel mementos—so they understand I won't need them, but they have a part of me and my joy. In do this I'm hoping to address the reality of "passing the wand."

Grief is when you are given time by others to readjust to your loss. The Dahlonega protocol served to expend much of Luther's wife's fright, anger, and abandonment she was feeling. After such a performance she probably got out of bed the next morning thinking "Thank goodness that's over!"

One English ritual permanently dented my friend who still shivers in horror at the memory of his father being sent down into whatever was behind the curtain. So I'm not sure that is helpful.

The Parsis seem to find closure having had several hours visiting with the departed.

The Saudi Muslim solution, so abrupt and bury before nightfall, is dictated by the Koran. Undoubtedly for sanitation reasons, but the tough love abandons any coziness.

I am giving my friends my adored collection of Imari blue-and-white pieces that I collected in Japan and that have been with me for thirty-five years. Friends were touched with tears. I explained the significance of the patterns and how difficult it is to paint on the biscuit,

Stevie celebrating life on her final birthday, November 6, 2007.

and that I wanted to give each person a piece whilst I was still able. That I hoped they would use them and think of me when they did. Close friends at a distance all want me to call them or come to visit just to hold my hand. It is very sweet and adorable to have so many willing and helpful friends.

I have had two letters this

week from my mother-in-law thanking me for loving Steve and giving everyone such a fun time and for pulling my weight in the family. It was very touching as it is deeply heartfelt from a very straitlaced, correct and emotionally restrained matriarch.

My dear mother has only me left, having lost her other children in their youth. She is settled in a very beautiful retirement home surrounded by friends and every day discovers more friends from the distant past in her yoga or aerobics class. I have always tried to be the dutiful daughter. Now of course I have to encourage her and spend time with her, but I cannot soothe her grief which is so bound up in my death, and so many other deaths, as well.

I have asked my friends to come to Nokomis, Florida, to be with me for a few days. It has been a good way for them to watch me deteriorate and for me to see them flourish. There are questions about the funeral and then one morning we talk about how death will be. Will it be nothing? Will it be full of a new kind of life? Will I try to communicate with the living? Will we care about the living at first or even later? I can tell them that for me I will simply go to sleep and it won't hurt; I just won't wake up. This is probably the most soothing fact I can relay. It is maybe the only fact known for sure. They treat me in a way that says I am already supposed to be the expert. But I am in the dark about any of the facts. Because I am on the team doesn't mean I already know the score.

Yesterday my friend Anne Fairbanks died of cancer. We had only met a few years ago, but always knew many people in common. We wrote e-mail and letters supporting each other. Anne was scared. I was able to make her feel better by telling her our grandparents would be waiting for us and our old family dogs. (Anne was a big lover of dogs.) She wanted so much to see the autumn again, and I am happy to think there was a bit of color on the trees for her to enjoy before she left this world. We talked about wanting something so monumental (like autumn colors) to happen just before we passed on. The best plans for a beautiful funeral were made by her husband, Tony, and his circle of people. It was sent out in perfect order. Then this morning a hurried e-mail arrived to tell us that the service time on Saturday was shifted fifteen minutes because it was St. Francis of Assisi's Day as well, and all the dogs were expected on the lawn for their yearly blessing. How wonderful a coincidence for our Anne to be asked to make a convenience for the canine community. She couldn't have enjoyed it more.

Encouraging my children to talk to me about death has become a strong focus for me. However, the other day Van (don't die, Mom) asked over the phone how I am. I said, "I'm fine. Boy, did we get a lot of rain from Gustav." He said politely, "Well, we can talk about the weather or we can talk about your health." It was only then that I began to see how I was sheltering Van from the facts and that I was the stumbling block. So I then reviewed at some length what the docs have said about my condition, what can be done, optional treatments—none—and what I am still able to do. Today I have worked most of sixteen hours on my three books and feel the same sort of accomplishment I have in the past. Plus, I have furthered two other little projects—finding out more about the ceramic porcelain painted by Auntie Cis at the turn of the last century and designing five little vignettes of antique items as a gift to the church's new gift shop.

One's energy is so unpredictable. To have gone fiercely all day could not have happened last week when I never seemed to rise above the loggie stage and lying down was more attractive than just about anything—except my beloved e-mail.

E-mail always gets me out of bed. I don't have a laptop. I have a control tower—an office in the middle of everything—and I do my work there. My friends are scattered to all the places we once lived and then on to their net posts and finally wherever they made their home—so anytime of day or night there is always a message of commiseration or encouragement. And one or three from my sweet cousin Glenice Mein whom I've never met. Glenice is the Head Girl of the Circle that researchers of family Mein join to compare notes and give clues on what they have found. Glen and I have become very close over two years. She is a great cheerleader and because she understands my time is limited has done a mountain of research for me as it relates to our James Mein b. 1833 who immigrated to Australia. She has confirmed the link, found his ship of immigration, and even met our relatives. That is the most wonderful gift to be given.

Three of us are to give a shower for a mutual friend's daughter who has the deliciously romantic name of Elizabeth Bennett. (If you go to the wedding page where brides register you will see three entries. Two are for Elizabeth Bennett marrying Mr. Darcy.) I e-mailed one of the others to say I think we should not plan it here because I don't know if my number will be up by then. She called me from her villa on Lake Como and there was nothing maudlin in her conversation. She was still the upbeat, creative pal I know. I love my friends who just stick to the topic and don't digress into discussions about how I'm doing. Don't get me wrong I like to be asked how I'm doing so I can say, "Just fine, thank you," like I do (cross that out) did the other day. That I can have challenges and good times with my friends who are not acting afraid of me or "the monster," as Glenice calls it, is a relief.

Today we lunch with an old friend who is a surgical doctor's assistant and her husband is a doctor and an old beau of mine. The conversation never left the realm of medicine. I wanted to tell my friend about how the children were doing. It was very tough for her to listen to as tears came to her eyes, which she wanted so desperately to disguise. I ended that conversation as soon as possible. Another day I had lunch with another friend and as I would rather talk about my children's reactions than facts about me, I did. As I spoke she listened intently as the tears fell down her cheeks. She never brushed them away . . . and perhaps she didn't know that they were there. Somehow it was easier to tell the story of the unfolding of my children's grief to someone so immediately present. Not that one should compare—both were loving expressions.

My recent life has been filled with the most wonderful nurses and doctors. They have cared for me beautifully and have told me that I am one of the family in hospital's Special Procedures Department. Today I was given a flashy fish cap of bold colors that I will wear for every procedure. Very exciting. The oncologist's office, too, is full of loving souls. They meet me with such friendship and love. Each department is full of darling folks who make one's visit joyful and often funny. None of these caring people would I have met if I had no cancer.

I would have missed the dearest friendships I've known for a very long time. So when my two-time survivor friend, Redenta Picazio, told me that even if she could, she wouldn't wish her cancer away because it made all of her life's blessings that much more precious to her, I listened. Yes, Redenta got it both ways—the full disease and the cure. By the nature of my cholangiocarcenoma there will be no cure for me. Redenta and I have a pact. I will pray for her forever if she prays for me forever. That's a pact I can live with.

Yet, the caring and nurturing spirit found in my caregivers has shown me a new kind of all accepting, nonjudgmental love. This love, though some might find it sort of academic in nature, has opened me up to passing this on to other patients in the waiting room, made me cognizant of shoppers having difficulty reaching a box too high, or aware of even someone who hasn't got enough wind to get to the door of the shop. I don't search for help. I find a place to sit with the breathless and then in a few minutes walk slowly out of the door together. I am not alone. This indeed is happening to all of us. This is growing in knowledge, patience and, yes, love until the day we die.

Ashley's Perspective

It is impossible to imagine life without you,
You are my best friend.
I feel that some events in life don't even occur until I get the chance to share them with you.

I will miss you desperately.

No one can replace a mommy, a best friend, and the person on the planet who understands me entirely.

There is no other family who has lived through all that we have.

None other that could understand the importance of what all of this international madness means.

I will think of you every time we drive to the Adirondacks and go through Malfunction Junction.

You will be with me when I take the bus to the Lower Lake, and I will feel you there as the awe of the view takes my breath away, as it does every time.

I will climb Indian Head and remember the time when we hiked up for fun and ran back down.

You will be in everything we do at the farm.

You will be with me when I shop for clothes, and when I wonder if that suits me or not.

You will be a feather in my hat; a pearl around my neck; the gold, rare, luxurious piece on my lapel.

You will be on my finger, wrapped around my finger.

I will sing all those Illahee songs to my boys and I will remember how we drove for hours and hours singing all those Illahee best hits.

Oh Birthday Queen.

If one day I will have a baby girl, she will come in your spirit, she will have your strength, your energy and your power.

I will walk through streets and look up for the detail and try and find you.

I will search for those tidbits of art history and information you told me as we explored London, Paris, Venice together. "What did Mom tell me?" I will wonder as I stop to look up at the clock on the Fortnum & Mason building in London.

I will ask you what that spoon is for or that bowl's purpose when I take out the serving plates at Christmastime.

I will wonder what color you would paint my front hall and what fabric you
would choose for the chair.
I will wonder where you are and what you are doing.
I will ask myself if you can see us and feel us.
I will find you in the butterfly.
I will see you in the mountain views and the feel you on the Key.

I will pray for you and I will ask God to send me signs that you are with me.
I will go to St. Mark's and belt out "Welcome Happy Morning" at Easter time
and "Angels We Have Heard on High" at Christmas. I will sing those
hymns with you.

I will try to do good and help and give and take care and guide and teach
and support and love . . . just like you do.

I will have learned about power. Power of mind and body and soul and spirit.
I will have learned about strength.
That in the past months, your physical strength has decreased and yet your
will has remained so strong.
That is an amazing example for me.

"Who will lead us? Who will love us in the way she did?" The answer is
no one. No one can love her children more than a mother.
I guess this is what I'm afraid of.
This Illahee piece of a song, replays constantly:
"Climb mountains while you may and sing your song
Start living every day
It won't be long before you turn around and wonder where life's gone"

Things I learn while going through Mom's jewelry:
Miss Venice charm
Dress-up jewelry
Antique Etruscan
Family emeralds
"STEVIE" in hieroglyphics
Collections of pearls, gold-dipped silver, Indian lacework

Archery medal pin
Gold and pearl pins from Onnie
Spaceship diamond ring, beam me up
You want everyone to have the perfect piece, the most appropriate,
    the best for each of us, meaningful.
Thank you for these precious gifts.

There's the cliché-but-true: your spirit will never leave me . . . you won't be
    gone, just away . . . I will hold on to all that you taught me, all that you
    gave me, all the simple womanly lessons, the social-intellectual insights,
    and the bigger wisdom about the world . . .

Our family is too young and you are too alive for all this finality. It's
    bewildering. And terribly unfair.

I am so sorry for your pain and all that you have suffered. It is impossible
    to believe that we are helpless now despite all that modern medicine
    has to offer.

Your book is such a gift—classic Mommy pushing herself 'til the end! It's so
    wonderful that you will share and document your varied experiences and
    profound insights into so many cultures. What a treasure you are creating!
    And it's so healthy to have a goal and project right now.

Never forget how angels surround you, fluttering and watching and healing
    and making sure it all unfolds as it should. These are challenges which
    seem too huge to us, but we only get what we can take . . . And we grow
    and we rise to the challenge, despite our broken hearts.

It is as it should be. No matter how tough. But it is so tough. And my heart
    will ache for you.

I will raise my children to be big and strong and interesting and bright.
    Never mediocre. Always asking questions. We will discover the world
    through travel and museums and books and movies. We will honor you
    by continuing so many traditions you started. They will be bold. Strong.
    Powerful. Like their Mamie.

Stevie and Ashley at Lower Ausable Lake, St. Huberts, New York, July 2008.

Hats Off to Stevie

Beau's Perspective

Mom's final wishes were, of course, well thought out and loaded with poetry, sweet irony, and symbolic tasks. The weekend after Thanksgiving, about a month after her death, Dad and I went out in a boat with our family pastor and two close family friends. Our instructions were to place her ashes in the Gulf of Mexico. Mom lived all over the world, and has seen every ocean from any number of shores, but her favorite body of water has always been the Gulf of Mexico. She was, in her own words, a 'water girl.'

When we got three miles out, our pastor committed Mom to the sea with prayers, and Dad put the low-fired clay folio containing Mom's ashes into the Gulf. It bobbed around a little bit and we sat in silence. I noted the cry of gulls, the water slapping against the sides of the boat, the brisk wind coming out of the West and the reflection of the sun, dancing upon the water.

I had three distinct observations as I stood there. First, I noticed how the folio was like a crab trap buoy, and I remembered sitting on my grandmother's dock with Mom as she explained how crab traps worked, and how crab trappers sincerely hate when people meddle with their buoys and traps. It was a sweet thought, and I relished it, as I hadn't remembered that moment in years.

Second, I noticed that the shape of the folio looked a lot like a docket of papers. I thought to myself that it was a folio of immense value, that documents cannot survive salt water, and that we were losing all of the insight and information that this extremely valuable folio carried. That was poignant.

We pulled away from the folio while it was bobbing about in the water, and made a slow arcing turn to the right. All of us held our breath as we moved off, hoping to see the moment when the folio finally sank beneath the waves. The sun's reflection, a cone of light, moved across the horizon and waves, and as we moved toward the shore, the folio passed into the cone of light. My third observation was the folio containing Mom's ashes crossing into the light on the water, and not coming out the other side.

Mom is gone. She is free: in Heaven, and in the sea, living within us even while we live without her.

Van's Eulogy

Good morning. Thank you all for joining us. I know my mother would be very pleased. I thought I would say a few brief words about my mother, who I loved and admired tremendously. I wanted to share with you some of the advice she imparted to her children on how to live life. Of course, by temperament, she had a wide range of strongly-held views. So I'll share just a few:

Growing up, Mom would tell us, "Whatever you do, be a great success or an outrageous failure – just don't be mediocre." She was telling us that the worst thing you could be was average. As a younger person, this did not make a lot of sense to me. In retrospect though, I think I understand what my mother's intent was. She was trying to equip us emotionally to take on risks and to have enough courage to live our lives in our own way. This also meant that we must strive for excellence. At the age of 10, Mom asked me if would be interested in studying art at one of the top art schools in London on weekends. In passing, she mentioned that this would involve drawing nude subjects. After I found out what that was, we both decided that I was a bit young for that experience. Mom was open to new ideas.

Mom also emphasized bravery. She really wanted us to take risks – lots of really good ones. My mother's travel itineraries were certainly a testament to this. Visiting us in Nigeria one Christmas, she impressed my embassy colleagues with her plans to drive through Mali and Chad with my father. No one in the embassy thought this was a good idea. Mali is a wonderful place, but the countryside is still a place of banditry and smuggling with pockets of religious militancy. But these concerns were not going to stop her from traveling to Timbuktu, which she had wanted to do for some time. Upon her return, it was clear that she was exhilarated from her trip. At the time, I didn't try to stop her from going because I knew she would find my interference very irritating. But when she announced her plans to travel to Iran while fighting cancer, I finally spoke up. I told her that the Iranian government was probably involved in kidnapping US citizens and that its nuclear infrastructure was going be bombed at some point. Mom was not impressed. She went to Iran anyway, a little miffed at my over-cautiousness.

Finally, she wanted us to be passionate about whatever we chose to do. She characteristically threw herself into the many, sometimes overlapping, commitments she made. This included her church, charitable organizations, associations, and the art world. Most of all, I think she was passionate about the people in her life, especially her family and friends. Mom spent a good amount of time each day writing or calling friends and family, which gave her great joy. She was particularly engaged when someone called her for help. She was exceedingly good at problem solving, and would deploy her enormous energies and intelligence into getting the thing fixed. This was all very reassuring – this was no longer just your problem; she very clearly saw the problem as hers too.

I miss my mom for her sense of fun, her big aspirations, her fierce loyalty and her zest for life.

Beau's Eulogy

Walt Whitman said,

> *"Each of us inevitable; Each of us limitless—each of us with his or her right upon the earth."*

I want to share with you what I see as an enduring facet of my mother's presence and that is her ability to inspire in others a sense of limitless possibility. She did it for me; she's done it for my wife, my friends, my boys.

I recall the night that she hounded me into acknowledging that **if I reached for the stars, I would get to the top shelf.** She just would not let it go until she was sure that I believed her. I did believe her. I still do

People who can inspire others to see their own limitless potential are gems among us: they are exceedingly rare and they shine so brightly.

So, I will strive to be that person now.

In my life, there is a hole I'm not sure I will ever fill. But I will try to rise above my worries and see what wonder the world has in store for me.

And I will endeavor to show my children and those around me the limitless possibilities that my Mom saw so naturally.

Steve's Eulogy

I will be very brief.

St Mark's is our second home. Stevie and I were married here 39 years ago, Ashley and Olivier were married here (Father Chris Gray even learned a bit of French for the occasion), three of our six grandchildren were baptized here. With all of the wonders of the world we have seen, this is our spiritual home, and this is where we will stay.

Stevie has always had a fierce pride in her children, not of arrogance but of willing them to excellence. She would be proud of you today.

Our last great trip was to Iran, just one year ago. We rejoiced in the cultural and spiritual richness of that ancient civilization. I close with a short poem by Hafiz, the 14th century mystic and poet whose tomb in Shiraz is a pilgrimage site. It is so perfect for Stevie.

> The God who only knows four words.
> Every child has known God.
> Not the God of names,
> not the God of don'ts,
> Not the God who ever does anything weird.
> But the God who only knows four words
> and keeps repeating them, saying:
> "Come dance with me."
> Come
> Dance.

Stevie's family also sang the song "Plant a Little Watermelon" at the reception after her memorial service, which is included below:

Plant a Little Watermelon

> Just plant a little watermelon on my grave,
>> let the juice (slurp, slurp) trickle through.
> Just plant a little watermelon on my grave,
>> thats all I ask of you.
> Well, I've tasted fried chicken
>> and it's mighty, mighty fine…
> But nothing could be sweeter
>> than a watermelon rind.
> So, plant a little watermelon on my grave,
>> let the juice (slurp, slurp) trickle through.

Stevie also had purchased hundreds of packets of watermelon seeds, which were given away like party favors to all who came.

Stevie and her brood, Summer 2006.

Front row (from left): Suki (Beau's wife), Van, Hannah (Van's daughter), Olivier (with son Hugo on his lap), Ashley (with son Theo on her lap), Yong Hea (Van's wife).

Second row (from left): Jake (Van's son), Jaxon and Julian (Beau's two sons).

Top row (from left): Steve, Beau, Onnie and Stevie.

Stevie's Life Travels

Stevie's International Travels—1960s

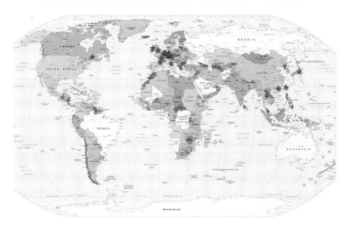

Ireland • England • Netherlands • Belgium • Luxemburg • Liechtenstein • France • Switzerland • Austria • Germany • Italy • Monte Carlo • Japan • Hong Kong • Thailand • Taiwan • Montreal (CAN)

1966 (May) Europe—Ireland, England, Netherlands, Belgium, Luxemburg, Liechtenstein, France, Switzerland, Austria, Germany, Italy, Monte Carlo.

1968 Travel with Nancy Clark and her parents to Asia: Japan, Hong Kong, Thailand, Taiwan (June). Meet Steve in Tokyo. Steve returns early December. Engaged at Christmas.

1969 (May) Marry Steve and move to Dahlonega. Canada on wedding trip.

Stevie's International Travels—1970s

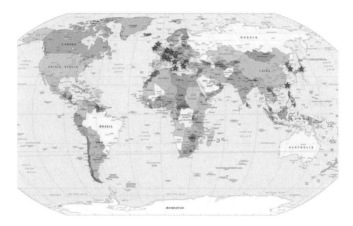

Ireland • England • Scotland • Germany • France • Austria • Germany • Italy • Monte Carlo • Japan • Philippines • Korea • Taiwan

1973–76 Move to Tokyo.

1976 Korea, Taiwan, Philippines, and Hawaii.

1977 Business trips to Austria.

1978 Business and art trips to Paris and Vienna. Spring in Rome and Pantelleria. Summer farmhouse in Kinsale, Ireland. Meet cousins in Germany with children and Mum. Stalking in Scotland.

1979 Art trip to Amsterdam. Business trips to Paris, Athens, Monte Carlo, and the South of France; Paris with Ashley.

Stevie's International Travels—1980s

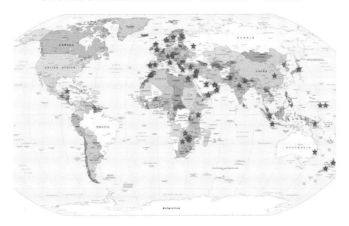

Scotland • Portugal • Russia • Japan • Italy • England • Austria • Saudi Arabia • Switzerland • Mexico • Austria • Morocco • Turkey • Greece/Crete • Syria • Jordan • Japan • China • Egypt • Nepal • India • Norway • Spain • Pakistan • Zimbabwe • Zambia • Botswana • Finland • Sweden • Yemen • Oman • Abu Dhabi • Singapore • Bali • Papua New Guinea • Australia • New Zealand • Tahiti • Bora Bora • Czech Republic • Slovakia

1980 Christies' trip to Scotland. The Algarve, Portugal. Tatoo in Edinburgh. Tokyo and Russia on business (September).

1981 (Spring) Rome and Castello di Gargonza with Onnie. *QE2* home after Royal Wedding.

1982 (June) London for Clare Clutterbuck's wedding and Vienna.

1983 (June) London, Wimbledon, etc.

1984 Two trips and a move to Riyadh, Saudi Arabia. Switzerland, Cozumel, Mexico (April). 15th anniversary trip on Orient Express to Venice (May); Geneva with Steve (July). Christmas Safari in Kenya.

1985 Skiing in San Moritz; London; Turkey, Istanbul, and Izmir (summer); Athens and Crete. Geneva (September). Christmas in Morocco.

1986 Spring in Venice and skiing in Cortina d'Ampezzo (Dolomites), and Rome; April trip with Mother to Istanbul, Syria, and Jordan. Drive in to Saudi. To Hassam. Japan and China and at the farm (summer); wedding in Copenhagen (September). Move to palace in Riyadh. Christmas skiing in Lech, Austria, and sail up the Nile in Egypt.

1987 To Hofuf, Saudi Arabia. Spring in Nepal and India; summer in Scotland, London, To London & Venice Oslo, Norway. Christmas in Spain with Mum.

1988 (Spring) Skiing in Zermatt, Geneva, Lyon, and Ajat at the Black's farmhouse; Eid in Pakistan—Karachi and Swat Valley; summer in Zimbabwe, Zambia, and Botswana, Egypt ;Sweden, Finland & Russia (October).

1989 Sanaa, Yemen, with Van. Move back to Greenwich, Connecticut via: Oman, Ab Dabhi, Singapore, Bali, Papua New Guinea, Australia, New Zealand, Papeete, Bora Bora. Ehrmann wedding in London (December).

Stevie's International Travels—1990s

BVIs / USVIs • Antigua • St Lucia • Barbados • England • Hungary • Israel • Hong Kong • China • Tibet • Austria • Russia • Italy • Corfu • Albania • Scotland • Wales • Germany • Capri/ Amalfi • India • France • Poland • Belgium • Holland • Singapore • Pakistan • Kyrgyzstan • Uzbekistan • Burma • Macau • Nepal • Canary Islands • Sri Lanka • Vietnam • Cambodia • Thailand • Finland • Latvia • Lithuania • Estonia • Denmark • Turkey • Bhutan • Malaysia • Indonesia • Corsica • Ireland • Borneo • Brunei • Lebanon • Syria • Cyprus

1990 Spring in Florida. Hungary, Austria, Czechoslovakia (Prague) and Bratislava, Berlin, and London.

1991 Caribbean cruise with Mum and Staleys (San Juan, St. Thomas, St. John, St. Martin, Barbados, St. Lucia, Antigua). London and Bath. London and Budapest (July). London and Lower Slaughter (October). To Israel on joint pilgrimage with Christ Church and Synagogue with Mum. Weekend in London (November and December). Sail with Fraser-Hopewells in Cornwall, Frenchman's Creek.

1992 (March) Central Europe, London twice. London (October), Hong Kong, China, Yangtze River, Tibet, with Mum visiting Ashley. Florida, London, Budapest, Vienna (November). London for ten days (December).

1993 B & S to London. Two weeks in London (January). Twice to London in February. Two weeks in London (April). St. Petersburg, Russia, for EBRD conference. Ten days sailing in Caribbean (St. Thomas to St. Lucia and all in between.) Fly to London and study New Testament through Renaissance Art in Florence (May). Meet Ashley in London (Sissinghurst with Harris) for 2 weeks (June). Concert at St. James's Palace with Paul McCartney. Meet Queen at Pilgrims. Corfu and then Albania for the Fourth of July. Meet Beau in London (July). Lake District. London for one week (September). Two weeks in London (October). One week in London. Edinburgh for Becky & Chris Main's wedding; mother & Jim Mein arrive. Connecticut for my fund-raiser for the Archbishop of Canterbury Dinner at the United Nations. Two weeks in London and my 50th birthday at Ottley Hall in Suffolk (November). 1 week London. London for ten days (December). Easter in Chester, England, and Wales.

1994 London for January and February. Family skiing in Garmisch/Partenkirken, and Munich (March). Amalfi coast, Pompeii, Capri, etc. (March). Fly to London, Bombay, and Hong Kong for four days each (July). London for ten days. Mum and I meet Steve in Bordeaux. Rent châteaus in Loire Valley and Dordogne. House parties in France. Fly to Warsaw for Rey wedding. Meet Beau, Katie, and Mum in Paris. Drive to

Belgium, Holland (September). London and 15th move into Ghia Mansion, Carmichael Rd., Bombay. London for three weeks. November birthday in Versailles. Bombay & Delhi. London and Hirtes for Christmas, Bayreuth for Wagner opera. New Year's with Coleridge in Devon, England.

1995 Bombay in early January. To Pune and Ahmedabad. Goa andCalcutta (February). London (March). On to Singapore and Hong Kong. Apl N of England in Langley Castle and Middlethorpe Hall. Bombay. To Udaipur and Delhi. One week in London (May). Bangalore. Fourth of July at farm. London and Bombay with Beau. To Jaipur and Mandu in the July monsoon. August Silk Road bus trip to Pakistan, Karakoram Highway, China, Kyrgyzstan and Uzbekistan. London and Bombay (September). Oct to Dungarpur, Trip to Burma with Bobo, Mandua for the day. London and spa at Englewood, fly to Bombay (November). Delhi and Palace on Wheels. Christmas in Cochin/Kovalam, rice fields and backwaters of Kerala.

1996 Lonavella with Piloo and Mum. London. Hambleton Hall in Oakham. Bombay. (January). Dungarpur. Madras and Hill Station (February). In March: With Indus to Varanasi, Khajuraho, Orchcha, Jansi and Gwalior. Hong Kong and Macau. Trip with Hirte children: Nagpur, Kipling Camp, Jabalpur, Pachmari, Bhopal, Bimetal, and Sanchi. Easter in Jersey; London, Milan, and Lake District; FL for a week; Bombay. Simla and HP; London and Connecticut (March). Party for Van and YH in London in April. Sept. London & Madeira. Meet Winnie & Jim—sail to Canary Islands. Fly to London. Nov. Mother comes to London and we fly to Grasse to visit Ashley, Janie G and her mother and sister. London. Bombay. Dec. To Maduri & Kodikanal. To Sri Lanka & Aurungabad, Delhi (Daulat Singh wedding.) Florida to New York City and London.

1997 Brussels to visit Belfrage. Bombay. February with Indus to Orissa. Mar. to Lucknow and Alibag Steve's 30th anniversary trip to Vietnam, Cambodia, and Bangkok. April to London, DC. June to Helsinki boat to St. Pete, Latvia, Lithoania, Estonia, Karliningrad, Poland, Germany, and

Denmark with Mum. Fourth of July at farm. Fly to London for parties. To New York City, Winnie's, Fisher's Island with Eleanor, Bombay. Farm. Aug to Amritsar and walk into Pakistan. Lahore to little museum with VC in diaries. Sept. Sail on the square rigger Odessa training ship on coast of Turkey. Oct train to Bangalore and Hospet and Hampi, Badami, Aihole, Belgam to Desais, Goa and Bombay. Delhi for BM party. Lonavella with Piloo. Bhutan, Darjeeling, Rumtek, Gangtok, Kalimpong, Sikkim. Nov. Indus trip to Saurashtra in Gujarat, Rajkot, last Pride of Lions in Asia, Diu, etc. Group weekend to Dungarpur with the one-hundred-mile traffic jam. London and Henlow Grange Spa; Florida for Christmas (December).

1998 Jan. Bangalore to Proutys & safari in Bandipur National Park and Mysore. Feb. Singapore with Harris, motor into Malaysia. Indonesian Spa with Selina Conner. across Java & meet Steve in Borabadur. Bali for Spice Island 4 day sail. Bangkok. Mar. Udaipur for Christopher Barrow's birthday. Mahabaleshwar Hill Stn. from Pune. April fly with Jaxon to Delhi. Easter meet Ashley in Corsica. To FL & NYC. London & Bombay. May Rajasthan trip with Phyfes. (Udaipur, Jodpur, Rohet, Deogarh, Kota & Bundi Jaipur.) Cochin w/e Residency & Coconut Lagoon with Fish. To Venice. June day in NYC buying loft. Curate our Indian Art Collection exhibition, Footprints of a Tryst, at The National Gallery of Modern Art, Mumbai. July Leave India via London: Henley with Flights, meet Ashley in Grasse, drive to Barcelona. To Brighton with Ehrmann for the day. W/e at Alborbugh with Flights. Aug with BM on Arthurian Legend trip to Cornwall, Devon & Brittany. Move to NYC. Farm. Sept Nantucket Botts wedding. Oct. Furniture/loft trip New York and Florida. Ashley moves to Beijing. November in Sri Lanka. December stop in Bombay. London for a week & New York. Van finishes Columbia. Florida for Christmas.

1999 Selling/buying real estate. Van et al in our loft in Union Square. January in Florida. Mayo Clinic. To New York City. Pack up Greenwich and drive to Florida (May). Hitchcock Film Festival at MOMA. St. Mark's reunion. London and Isle of Wight (June). Circumnavigation with Mum of UK: Isles of Scilly, Wales, Ireland, Isle of Man, Orkneys, Herbrides, Shetlands, Edinburgh; Hirte, drive to Alsace Lorraine; Coleridge in Devon; sailing with F-H in Ireland (July). Farm in August. September/October trip with Steve to San Francisco, Vancover, Beijing, Hong Kong, Sarawak, Sabah, Borneo, Brunei, Singapore, Bombay and then first Phoenician trip: Lebanon, Syria, Cyprus. Sold London house. Buy and move to Weyerhauser house on Casey Key, Florida (Van, too). Sheila and Dick visit Casey Key. Christmas in Florida. To New York City for final fling in our flat.

Stevie's International Travels—2000s

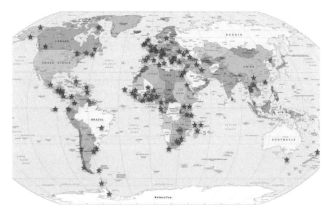

England • Greece • Turkey • Bulgaria • Ukraine • Russia • Georgia • Italy • Austria • Switzerland • Germany • France • New Zealand • Tasmania • Hong Kong • Laos • Thailand • China • Tunisia • Malta • Sicily/Sardinia • Antarctica • Brazil • Guatemala • El Salvador • Honduras • Belize • Sweden • Guinea • The Gambia • Senegal • South Africa • Lysotho • Swaziland • Namibia • Colombia • Ecuador • Galapagos Isl. • Madagascar • Mauritius • Iran • Turks/Caicos • Uruguay • Argentina • Falklands • Chile • Mexico • Spain • Costa Rica • Scotland • Canada • Nigeria • Cape Verde Island • Senegal • Mali • Niger • Burkina Faso • Ivory Coast • Ghana • Togo • Benin • Gabon • Cameroon • Kenya • Uganda • Tanzania • Seychelle • Sudan • Egypt

2000 New Millenium in New York City Times Square, Chrysler Building gargoyle floor party; Met Opera Der Flaudermouse. Van et al move to Washington, D.C. February: New York City. Father's stroke here and Jet ambulance. March to Savannah for Bobo's house party. Mom's siege in theater. April to NY. Chase Wildlife Foundation Benefit. To London. Dinner and luncheon parties with friends during which Julia arrives during lunch from her long drive across Iran and Turkey in the Fiat. May: sail with Harvard in Black Sea: Greece, Turkey, Bulgaria, Ukraine, Russia, Georgia. London and Florida. Drive north visit Van in Virginia, New York and fly to London. July to Rome and drive to Spolito, San Marino, Verona, Salzberg. Innsbruck, Lucerne, and Darmstadt. Drive with Hirte to Champagne and vineyards and Uncle Gus' grave. Paris and NY. Farm. August: Glimmerglass. I fall on stairs and break my foot. November: Fly to farm. Father dies and we fly to New York. December: London for a week: BM Great Court "chad" party. Fly to New Zealand for Winnie's Millenium birthday. Sold New York City, Greenwich, London, and Eagle Point. Plan to build new house at farm.

2001 Millenium January: Winnie's 60th in New Zealand: Tazmania, Hong Kong, Kunming, Laos Thailand. London opera. Mar. with St. Mark's church "In the footsteps of St. Paul" cruising in the Mediterranean with Mum. Las Vegas to Nashville. New York, Burlington, Florida. In June drive Glacier National Park, Yellowstone, Dude Ranch. Suki's stroke. Drive north visit Ives, Outer Banks, Van, Pam & Piers' wedding in Warren, Pennsylvania. July: fly to Beijing. Cooperstown-Glimmerglass. Aug: Saratoga with Wilds. Fly to Florida. Mother has gall bladder out and Suki has brain surgery. Back to farm. Fly Sept. to Brittany (Brest) to meet the Balavoine. Ferry to Plymouth. See Tigger's Mrs Astor's House & Coleridges for possible wedding sites. Party at Lushes for Ashley. Overnight at Julia's. Meet Hirte and drive to Dresden. Second Phoenician trip: 9/11—Tunisia, Malta, Sicily, and Sardinia. Farm. Christmas in Florida. Bruce built road, but we decided not to build on mountain. Start renovations at farm. Join board of Prosperity Rings.

2002 Steve's 60th birthday voyage to Antarctica, Brazil, Uruguay, Argentina, Falklands, Chile. May: New York, Ausable Club; Mexico with wedding gifts; Washington, D.C. Drive Outer Banks and Eastern Shore, Maryland. Greenwich parties. Farm finished. Cooperstown and Glimmerglass. August: NH Brownlie & Portland to Pink. Saratoga Races. Aug. Colorado at Dominick Ranch, and Santa Fe, New Mexico. Aug. fly to Blessing in Morlaix. Drive to Campair and south through western France, Bilbao, Spain, and northeast England. Hamptons at McKenneys, Mt. Kisco.

2003 February: birding in Costa Rica. April: birding in Arizona. Drive to Mexico with wedding gifts. Stay with Diane & Robert in Texas. Drive to Arkansas, fly to New York City for party. June to London: with St. Mark's church to Cathedrals in England; Scotland, Bute house party, Devon and Quintocks with Coleridge, overnight Cockings; study the Olympians at BM in London with Francine. Steve drives north with Yong Hea and children. Farm. July: Mexico. Drive to Georgian Bay Canada with Eliz and Lionel Smith and to farm. A week in Washington, D.C., with Hoopers whilst we get our African visas. My 60th birthday trip to Africa (November November '03–February '04: Nigeria, Cape Verde Island, Senegal, Mali, Niger, Burkina Fasso; Ivory Coast; Ghana.

2004 Togo, Benin, Gabon, Cameroon, Kenya, Uganda, Tanzania; cruise to Zanzibar, Comoros Islands, Seychelle; Sudan, Egypt, Sinai, London. In March overnight in Ft Myers with Bishops & Mystery Train. Pasternaks here a week for 3 35th wedding anniversaries. May fly to DC to buy a new house for Van. Tallahassee for CEO's dinner at FSU and Cedar Key. Drive to Naples overnight with Leibs. Three days in Key West by Hover Craft from Ft Myers. Drive N thru Georgia and NC stayed for ten days with friends discovering why people retire there. July Farm. VAB et al for the month. Aug. to Northeast Harbor , Boston, Fly to Ireland, N. Ireland, London and Lincolnshire in August. Beau moves to Phoenix; St. Mark's Reunion in CA. Reunion with Texas cousins in San Miguel de Allende. Ashley's cyst surgery. I stay on. Fly to meet S in DC and overnight with Van et al who move to Guinea. Four Hurricanes.

2005 Jan fly to NYC for Jack Bishop's funeral & MMA shows stay with KVCW with flu. Snowy Feb. day in NYC to visit Christo in Central

Park. To Phoenix with Mum & S to visit Beau et al. March to Central America for birds & Mayan ruins: Tikal, Copan et al in Guatemala, El Salvador, Honduras and Belize with Ashley et al. Chair WPHS "61Reunion Comm. Film video with Bill Schwartz. Join board of Historic Spanish Point. Ashley, Olivier & Hugo and Beau visit in May. Lucy Moore comes to speak and promote her book. Quick overnight trip to NJ to help A&O find a house to buy. June to England visiting Mein relatives & on to Venice Bienniale with official party of Museum of the American Indian. Drive north thru WVA filming with the Wares. House party July 4 Smith, Evans, Viccilleo. Alaska cruise to Artic Circle, Victoria with Narwani, glass train to Lake Louise and Banff. Gusti, Utah and NM & Arizona- Beau's graduation. Farm. Sept. Mother's seizure. Sotheby's sale of Indian Paintings. Trip to Great Lakes & Oct. Chicago to Doug's with Mum. Nov. fly to Stockholm for w/e for Anna Mosesson's birthday. Dec. Africa via London, to Ehrmann's 50th. Paris, Conakry, The Gambia, Senegal, South Africa, Losthoto, Swaziland and Namibia.

2006 Jan return from Africa. Weekend in NJ end of Jan visiting To Mt Kisco & NJ end of March (BM dinner at MMA, April Ran WPHS 45thReunion. Present class video "45 for the 45th" with Bill Schwartz. Together it seems like a self-actualization a la peak of Dr. Maslow's pyramid. To Ashley for birth of baby. Adopt Olaff, elephant in Ambroseli Park. May to Bogota, Colombia to visit Tica and John via Panama City and Cartegena, Col. And a week in Quito, Ecuador & Galapagos Is. with Mother and Sheila Clark. June Jaxon comes here alone for fishing summer camp. Cooperstown parties, Boston Gavin Gilmor 65th, to Winnie, Lucy, Riki in Portland ME, Nova Scotia, PEI, New Brunswick, & Gastronimical trip thru Quebec. To FL 3 days July& Aug. Read at Am Art Library DC. Stay with Van who doesn't move to Lagos. They move to CK& interviews. Sept London Sam Clark wedding, research Gibson relatives, Danube River trip from Black Sea. Coleridge farewell to house & Sale. Give Mother's 90th birthday party. Birding 3 weeks in Nov Madagascar, Mauritius, Rodriques and Reunion Is. Dec. Publish The Master of North Point.

2007 To Mt Kisco for Mother's birthday, gave party. Weekend in Atlanta helping V&YH find a house to buy. Visit Perk in Birmingham & help Van move into new house in March. To Galbreaths in Jupiter. April alone to England: Coleridges, Halls & Sargents for five exhibitions, research, and Anna's new restaurant. Discovered bile duct cancer, returned to Florida, Dr. Loewe put in stint; to Boston April 30 with Mom and Steve for Theo's birthday party, then all to Boston for operation—two weeks in Mass General and one week at rehab. Return to Florida. Chemotherapy and radiation all of July. VAB et al to Florida for two weeks July: sailing and zoo camps. Fly to farm for two weeks Aug. Smiths, Sheila & us to Cooperstown. Home 1 wk, Sept. fly to Seattle visit Sharp in Puget Sound, Christoffersson in Portland, Oregon Shakespeare Festival, Moss in N.CA And San Francisco for Comm Foundation conference. Sept Steve teaches at FSU & visits Mt Kisco. Oct to London and Persia with the MacDonalds, back to London with Wendy. Birthday drinks party at Wendy's. Home for hernia repair; buy yellow Crossfire. Give Persian party, back in hospital the next day with jaundice amd two procedures. Dec. 22 Botts wedding NYC, Christmas with Sheila & Smiths in FL. I miss due to flu. New Years' cruise: Cancun, Cayman Islands, Turks, Caicos, and Bahamas.

Missed: Point Pelee, Spoleto Festival; Bruce Museum benefit; Peru, North Carolina condos.

2008 Resigned from HSP board. NOT accepted. Worked on luncheon as Honorary Chair on January 28. Five days in Boston at Mass General. Tube replaced. Hear Geraldine Brooks speak. Marj. North does article on yellow Crossfire. Steve speaks at Glenridge about Persia (January). Venice Hospital in/out many times (February and March). Mar to Julia's & then John Plant's 80th birthday and abort trip to Oman. Recover at Sheila's. Drive north taking Beau's boys to Atlanta. Return to London to research Main/Spoor family in July. Four days at farm in August. Gave trip to South Seas to Glenice and Allan Mein.

LIVING ABROAD

BOMBAY, INDIA

By Ann S. Spaulding Wilberding

NEARLY 200 YEARS BEFORE WE MOVED TO Bombay, several of my husband's Van Cortlandt ancestors had settled in India. These were sons of Philip ("the Loyalist") Van Cortlandt, who had chosen the losing side during the American Revolution and had to leave New York just ahead of mobs bent upon tarring, feathering and lynching. Many Tories sailed with the defeated generals Cornwallis and Howe when they returned to England via Nova Scotia in 1783. Two of Philip's sons had died as infants in the New World, but his three surviving sons all took commissions in the British Army, as there wasn't much left to inherit.

Jacob eventually died in the Peninsular War in Spain in 1811, but Henry Clinton served in Northern India as Lt. Col. of Her Majesty's 24th Foot (later to become the South Wales Borderers) and married an Afghani tribal princess, while Arthur Ahmuty died as a captain in the 8th Native Indian Regiment in Madras.

Henry Clinton Van Cortlandt had one son, Henry Charles Van Cortlandt (1814-1888), who became General of the Punjab Army and for thirty years played a critical role as political advisor and kingmaker of Nawabs. In 1857, during the Indian Mutiny (or the first Indian war of inde-

pendence, as the revisionists would style it today), Henry Charles kept his army faithful to the British, and pacified Haryana State, which surrounds Delhi, the northern capital. His style presaged that of Gen. Sherman marching through Georgia only a few years later.

While Henry Charles eventually returned to England and died there in 1888, his children apparently remained in India. The records of the British Library in London are silent after the baptisms of their seven children, but one day we hope to go to Lahore, now in Pakistan, to find the old Army records. This could well lead us to a number of cousins in both Pakistan and India.

On arrival in Bombay in Autumn 1994, we had a well-honed moving plan intended to bring our household goods through customs quickly. But as we stepped into the airport the newspaper headlines were screaming "Bubonic Plague!" Airlines canceled flights in and out of India, and our pusillanimous container ship company panicked and parked our containers in the Emirates. It was quite a welcome, but after a full two months our furniture at last caught up with us in a plague-free city.

We came to Bombay well prepared for challenges, in both work and personal living, having not only survived but enjoyed living in Saudi Arabia, Japan, and England several times, as well as having travelled and worked in many of the newly emerging markets of the world. My husband, Steven, also had what he regarded as the best preparation of all for this pioneering work: he was Pathfinder Officer for the 101st Airborne Division in South Vietnam during and after the 1968 Tet Offensive. But Bombay has proved to be the most interesting challenge yet.

The people who live here like to say that Bombay is to Delhi what New York is to Washington. That is, the one is the business and cultural center, the other the political. Bombay has also always been home to a host of foreign arrivals — starting with the Parsees from Persia and later the Portuguese. It's a tough city: tough to negotiate and tough to manage. No one is lukewarm about it either — it's love or hate. Those who love it can see beyond the littered streets, the homeless (65% of the population), the congestion, the pollution and the beggars. The indi-

genes are themselves mostly from somewhere else in India or the sub-continent, or recently repatriated after several generations in Africa or England.

One shops at Crawford Market, the local "supermarket," with individual stalls in sections selling fruit, vegetables, flowers, baskets, metal crockery, paper goods or imported foods. In the parking lot Henry, our

CLOCKWISE FROM TOP LEFT: SCULPTURE, KHAJURAHO; PAN STREET SELLER; ELEPHANT MARCH, KERALA; DISTINCTIVE BOMBAY ARCHITECTURE AND TRAFFIC. PREVIOUS PAGE: THE PRINCE OF WALES MUSEUM

driver, and I are accosted by bearers with wide shallow baskets in which they can put your purchases to carry on their heads — the local answer to the shopping cart. Inside the door several unsavories vie to sign on as guide or translator, pushing official-looking badges in your face and shouting, "Licensed, licensed!" It is best to hire

one of each, otherwise you proceed around the acre of covered market (above with tin and below with straw) with a small entourage of fist-shaking indigents. First to the fruit section. When you want oranges you ask for "sweet lemons," and you say "oranges" for tangerines and "lemons" for limes. But limes are considered a vegetable and aren't found with the fruit. It turns out they aren't really a vegetable either, but are around the corner from the vegetable section where one man has the monopoly on them. Then to the imported goods. One goes from stall to stall asking for, let's say, Hellman's mayonnaise. The closest we get is a squeeze bottle of Hellman's Light. I'd never seen one before! Twelve tries later I come up trumps with plastic cups. Later we are stuck in traffic behind a truck advertising: "PEPSI, artificially flavored. Contains no fruit or pulp." It's then that I ask Henry why "lemons" are a vegetable.

"Well, they are used as pickles, in curries and vegetable dishes, squeezed on everything but dessert."

It made me scratch my head, wondering why *we* think they *are* fruit!

What isn't bought in stores, bazaars and markets will be brought to you. People pushing peacock fans to tourists on the street are legion. The hitch is that they can't be exported and are confiscated at the airport. (No doubt Customs sells those plumes back to the pushers.) One can buy any of twenty different magazines or newspapers at most traffic lights from the same boys who used to beg at that corner. Vendors visit you at home. Yesterday afternoon, for example, the following appeared at our door: a Kashmiri carpet dealer; a trio of carpet makers (dhurries or knotted carpets to order) with pictures and order forms; the lobster seller, sent up to us by a friend, with a bucketful; two newspaper deliveries; the milk lady; and a belated request for Christmas bakshish from the telephone company boys — who were sent packing as they had already got theirs at Dewali (Hindu New Year).

Along Carmichael Road, our residential street, parades a procession of craftsmen: the barber and the knife sharpener on their weekly progression of sales locations; the bed maker strumming the taut strands of bed rope to announce his arrival; the dancing monkeys leaping to their trainer's drumbeat. And on the occasional Sunday, an elephant slinks up and down the thoroughfare. (Slinks? Ah, yes — Indian women are told to cultivate the beautiful walk of an elephant!) And we were recently pleased to see a new shop had opened up around the corner: King Kong Beauty Parlour. On one occasion as we walked by, a snake charmer called to us, "Come have a look. These are good cobras, from Bombay, not Delhi." His claim was later confirmed during a trip to Delhi when, at Qutb Minar, one charmer lifted the lid from his basket and a *long* cobra jumped out and slithered down the path. The other cobras stared after him but were too lethargic to follow, which was just as well as the charmer had his hands full. I personally didn't stick around to see what happened.

In the business district one walks in the street because the pavement is jammed with entrepreneurs more numerous than on Carmichael Road: the man sitting with his typewriter ready to compose letters for the illiterate, the coconut milk salesman, the cobbler, a barker with a makeshift ferris wheel with four seats, and the maker of paan (lightly narcotic dinner mint equivalents). In the morning the street dwellers get up and do their ablutions at the spigot on the pavement, and can be seen busily washing their teeth and bathing, having already folded their blankets and stowed them in a tree. There are many sleeping in the streets, but their needs are provided for and they don't freeze in Bombay. One can

buy a variety of food from stalls on wheels. A man sells tea and rolls along the pavement each morning. Here "homeless" doesn't mean "jobless": the street dwellers usually have some basic manual-labor job or are self-employed in some form of hustle.

Begging is as prevalent here as in London and New York, but more persistent. At nearly every red light a family taps on the car window asking for a rupee. They persist as if alms are a divine right, and will badger until traffic moves on or a coin is proffered. There are also waves of postcard and magazine sellers. It is pointless to indicate a polite "no." Any reaction, even to say "no," is viewed as the first step

In the traffic pecking order, cows come before trucks

of negotiation. (Instead of giving, our driver Henry and I work at a school held under a tree in the median of the airport road, teaching English and soccer to the most eager of students.) Near home, there is a woman who begs for a coin to buy milk for her snake, which she keeps in a bread basket. Henry says she's pretending there is a snake, but one day she really had one. I always lock the door as she looks vindictive!

Of course cows wander everywhere and are looked after by all because they are symbolically associated with Lord Shiva, the greatest god in the Hindu pantheon. Some cows are on leads tended by old women who feed them a handful of greens for every coin received from a passerby. In the traffic pecking order, cows come before trucks — the only exception to priority by size. Therefore, we must wait for the untended cow to stir her stumps on any highway. Taxis sometimes give her little bumper nudges. Nonetheless, all must circumnavigate the cows luxuriating in the fast lane, or sleeping dogs who've claimed a cool patch not exactly on the side of the road. I will say

this about Bombay though: they've drawn the line at allowing pigs to forage on the streets, as porkers do in other towns in India.

We've joined the Willingdon Club for golf and tennis. Half of the courts are surfaced with cow dung and our most pressing rule is "Don't lick your lips when you serve!" During monsoon the backcourts are a little slippery. The newly all-weather-surfaced courts have brought a more cosmopolitan air to the sport, and now the ball boys and the markers wear tennis shoes. The club also has an excellent library of out-of-print books.

There are now fewer and fewer Caucasian foreigners here, because of the high cost of living (the highest rents on earth are in Bombay), and because more Western-educated Indians are now willing to return to India. We remaining foreigners live very well, however, usually with staff and spacious accommodations. And one can usually find a kindred soul with whom to tap dance, speak Italian, learn the oboe or travel about the country. We form clubs to learn about our hosts' culture and to keep in touch with our own. There are differences which frustrate to distraction even the calmest of us: the occasional 25-minute wait for a dial tone, the fifteen-day wait to have the (fill in the blank) repaired, or the cataclysmic fiascoes when certain requests are misunderstood. One eventually reaches one's threshold and goes berserk, alas, but invariably at the wrong time. The other day, on a tour of a weaving factory in Aurangabad, I noticed that the women tended their looms in dim light, and I refused to continue the tour because it was "horrible for management to strain their employees' eyes. The management should get lights...blah, blah." The manager, more politely than I deserved, apologized and said, "Sorry, Madam, we have a power cut today," and pointed to the many darkened overhead lights. We can never hope to assimilate the all-pervasive spirit of tolerance and compromise that is the salvation of India.

From November to April all foreigners have houseguests — loved ones from

THE BANGANGA FRESHWATER TANK WHICH FIGURES IN THE EPIC, *RAMAYANA*

home, business people who are tired of hotels, backpacking nieces and offspring of friends-of-friends — thrilled at the prospect of a shower and a Western refrigerator, to say nothing of soft beds. Evenings have two phases: cultural programs start at 6:30 and dinner parties after 8:30. Entertaining is done in wonderfully elegant locales with exotic food and absolutely fascinating people. Rarely do you meet an Indian professional who doesn't have another vocation

MR. AND MRS. WILBERDING

— artist, playwright, concert pianist. Conversation is always cheerful and accommodating and often something arrives at your door the next morning to follow up on a meeting of the previous evening. There is a total absence of cynicism, and honest sympathy isn't a stranger here.

Until last year it was rare to find any but the locally manufactured cars on the streets. "Ambassadors," whose frame approximates a 1950 Desoto, or the popular "Maruti," a small 80s Japanese sort of design, have little power, which fortunately keeps traffic to a slow pace. Three lanes become six during rush hours. A friend explained that there are only two rules to driving: 1) the larger vehicle has the right-of-way and 2) use your horn to communicate with those in front of you (i.e., when you want them to move, alert them that they have a flat or that the baby fell out of the window). Trucks, all with "Honk Ok Please" on the back bumper and belching black smoke, naturally have the supreme right-of-way.

Despite the poverty and crowding, however, one feels safe on the streets of Bombay. There is crime, but violence is mainly within the family: crimes of passion and dowry crowd the front pages. However, a recent new scam begins at the international airport where thugs scout Indian passengers coming off flights from the gold market cities of the Middle East. The passenger with the most luggage is followed on the highway into town where, just in front of a hospital, his car is forced off the road. Windows are smashed by waiting thugs who drag the people out, cut one of them and make off with what they hope is a cache of gold. The shocked and defiled bundle into the hospital, declaring that they've had an accident. If they report it as a crime they won't receive treatment until the police investigate. Of course, the thieves count on this to give them an extra hour or so to disappear. For the most part we feel pretty safe though.

So, while there are frustrations, and we occasionally yearn for the A&P, autos with a lot of horsepower and friends and family, all those are in a place where you have to carry your own bags and where a day's outing is not nearly as interesting. ■

About the Authors

Stevie and Beau, 1978. This picture says it all!